EXIT FROM WORK

What Will The New You Look Like?

GREGG LUNCEFORD, PH.D., CFP®

EXIT FROM WORK:
WHAT WILL THE NEW YOU LOOK LIKE?

By Gregg Lunceford

ISBN: 978-1-944027-39-1

Copyright © 2020 by Networlding Publishing

www.networlding.com

All rights reserved.

DEDICATION

This book is dedicated to my wife, children and others who inspired it.

TABLE OF CONTENTS

Preface 1

Chapter 1: A Redefinition of Retirement and the 10 Myths 7

Myth 1: My Employer and Social Security Will Provide for My Retirement 14

Myth 2: My Inheritance Will Provide for My Retirement 15

Myth 3: Medicare and My Employer Will Provide for My Healthcare 17

Myth 4: My Spouse Will Provide for My Retirement 18

Myth 5: My Lifespan Is 75 to 85 Years 20

Myth 6: Safe Investments Such as CDs and T-Bills Are All You Need 20

Myth 7: You Should Retire at Age 65 21

Myth 8: Retirement Planning Is a Financial Exercise 22

Myth 9: It's Easy to Retire from a Career or Profession 23

Myth 10: We Only Have to Plan for Ourselves in Retirement 25

Summary 26

Three Action Takeaways 29

Chapter 2: What Is Work? 31

Why Is It Good to Work? 42

Fired into Success 43

Amazing Senior Entertainers Who Continue to Inspire Us 49

Why Work May Not Be Good 52

Three Action Takeaways 55

Chapter 3: Is Retirement Broken? 57

The History of Retirement 61

The Formation of Retirement in the U.S. 62

The Modern View of Retirement 66
Three Action Takeaways 70
Chapter 4: What Do You Want Exit from Work to Be for You? 73
Finding Number One 74
Finding Number Two 78
Finding Number Three 81
Finding Number Four 84
What Are People Looking For? 85
Three Action Takeaways 86

Chapter 5: Reclaim Your Life 89
Having It All 90
What Should You Do with Your Life Bonus? 92
Moving from Money to Mission 106
Three Action Takeaways 111

Chapter 6: Laddering Bonds and Buddies 113
Historical Family Structure 117
Your Best Network Is the One You Create 120
Three Action Takeaways 129

Chapter 7: Discovering Your Financial Strength 131
Do I Have Enough? 143
Financial Self-Efficacy 146
Increasing Self-Efficacy 149
Three Action Takeaways 153

Chapter 8: Exit Options 155
Going Back to College 156
Internships or "Returnships" 157
Peace Corps 158

Entrepreneurship 159
Restructuring Work 161
Three Action Takeaways 163

Congratulations on Being More Exit-Ready! 165
Before You Go 171
Notes 173

PREFACE

I've been in financial services for over 25 years. During my career, I've worked with clients on a wide range of financial topics, from corporate and investment banking to wealth management. In my industry it is often believed that a person's decision-making is largely influenced by their economic options. As a financial planner and wealth manager, one of my biggest assumptions was that individuals will exit work when they can afford to leave. This assumption is widely held in our industry and can be seen in advertising by many financial services companies where the main focus is on how much money you will need in order to stop working.

Growing up, stories about work did not seem pleasant when I talked to older people in my community. Many people I knew had blue collar jobs that were mentally and physically stressful such as housekeeping, construction, or manufacturing. The message to my generation from older workers was clear: "Go to school and get a good education so you can have a great job that leads to a career."

When I finished graduate school and started working, I noticed older professionals frequently talked about how they could not wait to reach their retirement date. They were going to have a big party, and if they wanted to, they could finally tell everyone what they were really thinking: "Take this job and shove it, I don't have to do this anymore." It seemed like work was a necessary evil—a means to an end—and most people could not wait to get to the end. This was a bit shocking to me because they had what was perceived to be good professional jobs. Growing up I thought people could not wait to retire because they were limited to less desirable work. However, I was hearing a similar sentiment from individuals who worked in prestigious organizations, held impressive titles, and received good pay and benefits.

My first full-time job was in a bank training program. The culture of the program included hazing and assigning the new trainees ridiculous tasks to see how thick their skin was. The behavior was justified by employees senior to us saying "cream rises to the top" and this was a weeding out process to promote the best people. I don't believe this is true, but that's a topic for a different book. On days when I was frustrated, older employees, many of whom had over 20 years of experience, would pull me aside and educate me. I had several, and my peers had their own mentors also, but the person that stood out the most was Cynthia.

Cynthia was an executive assistant in her late 50s. She was hired after high school and knew everything and everyone in the company. She was not a busybody and learned by observing others' behavior. It was clear she was one of the smartest people in the company. Cynthia had raised her own children, and trained a few executives as if they were her children. When I was having a bad day and feeling frustrated with someone she would say, "I remember when that person was a trainee—they were awful and got promoted from the bottom of their class." She would go on to explain any stories the person told about their greatness as a trainee were only illusions in their mind. She would also inspire me and others to continue on. However, the main reason she would give us to continue had to do with retirement. Cynthia and others like her would always make the argument that you should never quit a job before you were vested in your company's retirement plan. No matter how bad work got, over time you would be the winner because you could eventually tell your employer what you really thought and they would still be obligated to pay your retirement benefits for the rest of your life.

I noticed this was not unique to my industry. When I talked to teachers, attorneys, police officers, physicians, and sales managers, all of them could tell me with some accuracy when their retirement date was and what their benefits would provide. It was common to hear someone say, "I have five years left and then I will receive 80% of the average of my highest four years of pay for life plus retiree medical benefits." I recall a story of an employee who did not keep track of his time and benefits. The legend goes one day he was in human resources asking an unrelated question and learned he was eligible to retire early with full benefits and a lump sum of cash. Within minutes of learning this information he announced his retirement and left the company a few weeks later. He was so happy I'm sure he forgot to tell a few people what he was really thinking, and instead took his check and ran.

As I mentioned, earlier in my career I viewed economic factors as the motivation for exiting work. However, during the Great Recession in the late 2000s I counseled several people who were offered great financial incentives to retire, but they were not happy and slow to take the bait. Unlike Cynthia and others, they were not excited to take the money and run. In several cases it took them up to a year to take the offer and finally transition from their employer. Although we quickly confirmed from our financial analysis that they could afford to exit work, it was not uncommon for them to request additional meetings to further confirm their ability to meet their lifestyle needs. In every meeting, they proposed new scenarios with dramatic downsides to be financially modeled, and in each case they had enough financial resources to be financially successful in retirement.

We were in the worst economic times since the Great Depression in the 1930s, so I understood their need to be cautious. However, I didn't understand why they were so unhappy and turned off by the opportunity to enter into a life of leisure. We were in a period where people were losing their jobs, watching their home values and investment accounts rapidly decline in value, wondering how they were going to pay for their children's education, and facing greater uncertainty. That being said, the individuals I was counseling were blessed to have more than adequate resources to sustain them for life, and in several cases, greatly benefit their children and grandchildren.

I began to question why people who were able to exit work were so unhappy, especially since they had financial security in such challenging times. Their behavior was the opposite of what my industry suggested, which was that people will opt to have a lifestyle of leisure when they can afford to do so. At this moment I knew there was something about the retirement process that I needed to understand. Something had fundamentally changed over the years; however, it was going unnoticed by many who were not immediately faced with a retirement decision. There was something about the transition and how it impacts people that was different than what their parents and grandparents experienced. I began to question what people think about and feel regarding exiting work and how their assessments may be different in the 21st century.

I entered a doctoral program and researched the process that people go through when they're considering the retirement decision. The goal was to figure out what it is retirees want in the 21st century and how that might be different, if at all, and to share those findings for the greater good. After well over 10,000 hours of study, reading, writing, exams, and research, I learned that exiting from work has gone from being routine to having a great deal of complexity for the 21st-century retiree. New retirees are faced with developing a strategy for success that considers increased longevity, fewer resources, and the potential for increased responsibilities. Because several new issues have not been experienced by retirees before us, many individuals are faced with developing a plan for success with limited points of reference to provide guidance.

Today's retirees will be pioneers and groundbreakers and will need to advocate for the lifestyle and freedom they want. Although this can seem frightening, the new retirement provides a life bonus where many individuals can experience the best time of their life. This book will explore exit from work in the 21st century to put it into greater context to help you develop a personal strategy for success.

CHAPTER 1: A REDEFINITION OF RETIREMENT AND THE 10 MYTHS

Every one of us, at one time or another, will leave our respective workplaces for one reason or another. Some departures will be planned, and others will not. But *where* we go after we leave and *what* we do is starting to look very different. I'm talking retirement. After extensive research and observation, I have a new name for the powerful shift and resulting opportunities that the nature of our world today, has brought to our doorsteps — *Exit from Work*.

What do we know about retirement? First, for many it's inevitable. Second, it occurs at any point in time. Third, it may be voluntary because you are tired of working or involuntary due to a layoff or downsizing. Fourth, it may be necessary because of your health issues or those of a loved one.

For instance, Jack (60) and his wife, Janet (65), had worked hard their entire lives. They saved up their money, and Jack went back to school to get certified as a massage therapist. It was, he told Janet, a way to make a living on the road. A former marathon runner, he knew there was a great demand at races around the country for an experienced massage therapist who either was or had also been a runner.

Janet, a receptionist at a local doctor's office, kept working. Their plan was to sell the house and move into their RV and travel once Jack graduated and got his certification. After two years of classes, Jack's graduation was only a few weeks away when Janet suffered a debilitating stroke. Her stroke and rehabilitation needs made it impossible for her to travel, even after her crisis was over. While their plans to travel had been suddenly and irrevocably changed forever, the good news was, they were somewhat prepared. Jack sold the RV and became the primary caregiver for his wife until she passed away three years later after another stroke.

Such stories aren't unusual. The statistics and stories about people who have heart attacks or strokes shortly after retiring have many retirees nervous about the day they are scheduled to retire.

But not everyone waits until they're 65 to leave the workplace. Today, more and more couples are retiring at age 40. Some are military veterans who have gotten their 20 years in and are able to stop working and look forward to travel and a modest retirement. Some start a business or seek a second career, and others pursue a life of leisure. The important thing to remember about retirement is it's not what it used to be: a lifetime at a company, a gold watch, and five years of watching television and gardening or playing golf.

Now, retirement can be a happy occasion as you shed unpleasant responsibilities, or it can be a sad transition as you let go of certain relationships: friends, colleagues, mentors, and others whose company you enjoy. Regardless of the reason, someday, you will retire, willingly, or not. That's a reality. As a result, you must decide what it will mean for you and how to manage the adjustment—when the time comes.

If you took the time to pick up this book, there is a good chance that you are self-actualized, and, as a result, looking for options and likely any new insights on how to do what I'm calling *Exit from Work*.

If you haven't heard this already, baby boomers represent one of the largest groups in the workforce. In fact, they have been turning 65 at a rate of 10,000 individuals per day for several years. Because of this dramatic exodus, life after work will be much different for them and those who follow than any other group that went before them. Unlike their predecessors, baby boomers will exit work with longer lifespans than ever before.

Right behind them there are 65 million people in generation X. There will also be a handful of millennials who have made their money in tech, or the gig economy and who plan to retire in their late 20s or 30s. For other millennials who have entered the workforce, once they enter that stage in their lives in three more decades, they may be a part of one of the largest cohorts ever to exit from work.

Men in their 40s can comfortably reach age 70. At 70 years old, the majority of men are expected to live another 10 years, and another quarter are expected to live to see 90. Women are generally expected to live longer lives than similarly aged men as they grow older. Women in their 40s can expect to comfortably reach 80, with many also expected to live until their centennial year. Even at 70, more than 60% of women are projected to live long enough to blow out 90 candles.[1]

To put it another way, these people are blessed with the best bonus of all—a life bonus. As a result, we now have a new normal where retirement age is occurring at middle age. In fact, 60 is the new 40!

There are additional statistics about increased longevity as well as some excellent strategic suggestions and models in the 2016 bestselling book *The 100-Year Life: Living and Working in an Age of Longevity* by Lynda Gratton and Andrew Scott.[2] The authors blended backgrounds in the fields of sociology, psychology and economics classify them as experts in the field of aging and longevity. The book provides broad, diverse insights and solutions on how to manage finances, education, relationships and career to live a productive, satisfying 100-year life. It also takes a look at what firms, politicians, governments and individuals must do in order to accommodate today's extended longevity expectancy.

Exiting from work may sound easy because it offers an opportunity to do less, but it also presents challenges that can be stressful for many people. Writer Sally Kane of TheBalanceCareers.com says baby boomers are extremely hardworking. They're motivated by position, perks, and prestige. They relish long work weeks and define themselves by their professional accomplishments. They also expect the same of those around them — regardless of their age. In fact, baby boomers may criticize younger generations for a lack of work ethic and commitment to the workplace.[3] Those traits can make retirement difficult for a variety of reasons, including mentally, financially, and emotionally.

Leaving one's current lifestyle and adopting a less supportive one can also prove very difficult. According to a 2013 study by the UK's Institute of Economic Affairs, retiring increases the probability of suffering from clinical depression by 41%. It also increases the probability of having at least one diagnosed physical ailment by 63%.[4]

For example, take the *Forbes* article that featured Dwayne, a Fortune 500 executive struggling with full-time retirement. The retiree complained of boredom, excessive sleeping, and other symptoms of depression after discovering life after retirement wasn't anything like he expected.[5]

After moving up the ranks of a Fortune 500 company to become company Vice President of Logistics, life without his career was a definite let down. After decades of being the leader his employees and staff looked up to, and having a full calendar of things to do and accomplish every day, now Dwayne mostly watched television or slept. Instead of traveling with his wife as he expected, she had other plans, which didn't always include him. There was nowhere to channel that energy, drive, and purpose he'd drawn on all his life. Small wonder he was depressed.

Similarly, there was the case of a 52-year-old family counselor and administrator who retired after 31 years of service, only to find herself bored and frustrated from lack of stimulation after just eight months of retirement. She later took a job editing books and went back to school. Subsequently, after returning to work she reported feeling "young, vibrant, alive, energetic and enthusiastic," adding, "I would like to work until I no longer can." These examples demonstrate an incredibly powerful shift in attitudes regarding work and retirement.

Although retirement presents challenges for many, it is still a dominant and preferred option over working a 9-to-5 job one hates. Ever-increasing numbers of people have been very successful choosing different options rather than retirement. Take, for example, stories of retirees like Jake Chesson, an avid cyclist who was featured in an article in *USA Today*. After decades of a lifetime enjoying cycling,

Chesson began to dread it. He knew if he didn't enjoy riding anymore, he'd stop doing it. So, he looked around for other options and found a Meetup Group of like-minded riders who combine their cycling with socializing. Now he enjoys both his riding and his social club, where he regularly participates in outdoor activities such as biking, hiking, and ice skating.

There are many people with stories like Chesson's who are looking at work they've always loved and done, but are now beginning to dread. They still have the desire, passion and ability to work, and want to do something meaningful. As a result, there is an increasing wave of people choosing alternative paths as they exit from the jobs they held throughout their traditional career span. Now, more and more people are successfully exiting from work into new careers or businesses that orbit more around their passions. They not only focus on their passions, but now have an increased desire to focus on making a *dent in the universe* as well. (à la Steve Jobs). These are the people I call *Thrivers*. I will talk about them extensively throughout this book. They are the new work pioneers who are essentially *redefining* retirement.

So, what is it about Thrivers that make them more successful at exiting from work than others? What can we learn from them? How are they redefining retirement? What can redefining retirement mean for you? How might you become a Thriver? Are you thinking about exiting from work in the near future? How do you feel when you think about retirement? Does the complexity of it scare you away from thinking about it at all?

Avoidance isn't a good strategy. The ocean's waves continuously ebb and flow no matter how deeply you bury your head in the sand. Avoidance often leads to greater complications over time. The purpose of this book is to help you better understand the changing dynamics associated with work transition and learn what may be possible for you. I'll share insights gleaned from extensive research and interviews with those who have approached exiting and those who have already exited from work *differently*. But before you set your course to exit from work, you must first understand what retirement is and isn't. Here are ten myths about retirement that will help you sort out your next move.

Myth 1: My Employer and Social Security Will Provide for My Retirement

Unless you've been in the workforce for a very long time with the same employer or you work in certain public sectors or union organizations, you may never experience a retirement pension, or a defined benefit plan as others have known them. That applies to the majority of people in the workforce today. Why? Old school retirement plans have gone the way of the dinosaur. Our companies no longer take care of us. We must take care of ourselves.

Today, fewer than 20% of companies have traditional pension plans that promise a lifetime benefit in retirement. Beginning in the late 1970s, the majority of such plans were slowly phased out in favor of retirement savings accounts such as 401k, 403b, and defined contribution plans that shift the financial risk of retirement to the retiree.

In addition, Social Security benefits are unlikely to cover your total annual expenses. Over the years, there has been debate over the longevity of the Social Security Administration system as it's currently structured. Even if it maintains, it's estimated that Social Security payments will replace only 40% of one's average household income. The percentage is lower for people in the upper income brackets and higher for people with low incomes.

You'll need to supplement your benefits with a pension, savings or investments.[6] If you are not already receiving Social Security benefits or are and want to learn more, you would be wise to visit the Social Security Administration's official website, ssa.gov.

Myth 2: My Inheritance Will Provide for My Retirement

An inheritance can make life easier, especially if you're fortunate enough to inherit cash. However, hoping to inherit money isn't a good retirement strategy. Why? The grantor of a gift can always change their beneficiary or marry someone who may take priority over you. In addition, the gift you inherit may not be as large as you think. After the estate settles its expenses and divides what is left among the beneficiaries, possibly including several individuals besides you and some charitable organizations, there just won't be the millions (or even thousands) you anticipated. Note that only 1.6% of heirs receive an inheritance over $100,000. Although this is enough for a nice gift, it might not be enough to finance your lifestyle in retirement.[7]

Eleanor, a talented CPA and an only child, expected to receive at least a half-million-dollar inheritance along with a $2 million home from her parents when they passed. So, she planned her retirement accordingly. Her savings, combined with her inheritance, would give her quite a comfortable retirement at age 50. What she couldn't foresee was both of her parents getting cancer within a few years of each other. Her anticipated inheritance was wiped out by exorbitant hospital bills and ultimately the placement of both parents into assisted living. The home had to be sold, along with the majority of her parent's assets. So, she obviously didn't get the house, and at the reading of her parent's wills a decade later, there was barely enough money left to bury them both and take time off from her job to grieve.

Life doesn't guarantee us anything. Fortunately, Eleanor was frugal, good with money, and had a well-paying job she loved. She was able to pivot and restructure her retirement by starting her own business.

Not everyone is so lucky. Most of us, 78% of us according to Forbes, live paycheck to paycheck. I'm not talking minimum wage jobs either. CareerBuilder.com conducted a survey and found that nearly one in 10 workers making $100,000+ live paycheck to paycheck. That's right. There are people making six-figures today who would be homeless if they lost their job tomorrow. The survey additionally revealed:

- Over 1 in 4 workers do not set aside any savings each month
- Nearly 3 in 4 workers say they are in debt - and more than half think they always will be
- More than half of minimum wage workers say they have to work more than one job to make ends meet
- 28% of workers making $50,000-$99,999 usually or always live paycheck to paycheck, and 70% are in debt
- Only 32% of the nearly 3,500 full-time workers surveyed use a budget and only 56% save up to $100 a month.[8]

Myth 3: Medicare and My Employer Will Provide for My Healthcare

Bill Jones, an active golfer and triathlete, retired early to pursue his love for sports, assuming his minor aches, pains, and injuries from his active lifestyle would be covered by

Medicare and his company health benefits when he turned 65. Along with millions of other retirees, Bill was in for a shock.

According to the Society for Human Resource Management's (SHRM's) 2017 Employee Benefits Survey Report, only 19% of SHRM member companies provide some type of retiree health coverage for their employees.[9] That number declined from 23% just four years prior. One strategy to deal with no retiree medical benefits is to retire after you qualify for Medicare. However, Medicare does not cover all health-related expenses such as long-term care and hospitalization in certain situations. Most times retirees must purchase supplemental insurance to cover gaps in coverage.

Elaine Jackson waited until she was 67 years old to check into Medicare, only to discover that by not signing up for health insurance within three months before or after her 65th birthday, she would have to have a medical exam to qualify for health coverage. If she had signed up within three months of her birthday she would have automatically qualified for health care and no one could have asked her any questions about her health or pre-existing conditions!

Myth 4: My Spouse Will Provide for My Retirement

Jennifer and Tyler, her husband, both worked full-time most of the 20 years they were married. Their marriage to each other in their 40s was a second marriage for both. Jennifer's husband was killed in Afghanistan, and Tyler's first wife died from cancer. They kept their finances separate, and the couple rarely talked about money, retirement, or the value of their retirement accounts. Jennifer assumed Tyler had some sort of life insurance benefits from his wife's death, and Tyler assumed Jennifer had military benefits from her first husband's death. Both were right — sort of. The money in each of their accounts was enough to take care of them for a year or maybe two, but not enough to retire on. Both had good jobs; both were putting money into their own 401k accounts, but neither knew how much they were saving, and just presumed it was "enough." Jennifer and Tyler aren't unusual. Money, retirement, and savings are difficult topics for many couples. Rather than have the "money" talk they assume that things are "okay," until they find out they're not.

Research shows that many times, couples are on different pages when it comes to saving for retirement. Although your spouse might be a good earner, don't assume a plan is in place to provide for you in retirement. In one study conducted by The Harris Poll, a research organization, of those individuals who reported their partner is saving for retirement, roughly one in five said they don't know how much their partner contributes to long-term retirement accounts or even have a general sense of the total value of their partner's retirement account. Other unexpected disruptors of your anticipated lifestyle might include divorce, a beneficiary change, or a reduction in benefits if your spouse passes before you.

Myth 5: My Lifespan Is 75 to 85 Years

"I really never planned to live this long," Mike, a condominium salesman, admitted. "Now I'm 63, making six figures, and I'm socking away as much money as I can. But the thing that bugs me is not knowing how long I'll live and if I'm saving enough. I'm guessing I have another 10 to 20 years, but who knows?"

The fastest-growing population age group is 85+. Because of this expanded lifespan, living to age 100 may become relatively common with all the developments in biotechnology, nanotechnology, and health care. Currently, individuals who reach age 60 have a 50% chance of turning 90.[10] Mike plans to continue selling condominiums as long as his health is good, but admits he's "not good with money," and isn't sure how to start, fund, and invest his money now so he won't be homeless in his 70s.

Myth 6: Safe Investments Such as CDs and T-Bills Are All You Need

As retirees in the 21st century are experiencing greater longevity than those before them, as stated above, it's very possible for them to have a lifespan that reaches age 90 or higher. A retirement portfolio built on treasury bonds and CDs made sense for earlier generations when life expectancies were shorter and inflation was tame, but that may not be the situation facing future retirees. A no-risk portfolio may well lead to the loss of purchasing power as you grow older and negatively impact your lifestyle in retirement. In addition, you may need to invest in other asset classes to compensate for income that once came from traditional pension plans.

Myth 7: You Should Retire at Age 65

After retiring at age 60, Hiromu Inada took up running to stay healthy. In 2018 he crossed the finish line of the 2018 Ironman World Championships in Kona, Hawaii, having completed the 2.4-mile (3.86 km) swim, 112-mile (180.25 km) bike ride and the marathon 26.2-mile (42.2 km) run in 16 hours, 53 minutes, and 49 seconds–just over six minutes before the 17-hour cut-off mark. In the previous Ironman, he missed the cutoff mark by just 5 seconds, so he was very pleased to have made a much better time his second go. Inada is not the exception to the retirement rule. Millions of seniors aged 60 and over are very active and involved and plan to stay that way into their 90s.

Somehow, this myth about needing to retire at age 65 has become an expectation or social norm. I'm amazed when I hear someone in their early to mid-60s share their age and the response from the person they are speaking with is "Oh, you must be getting ready to retire." Retirement at age 65 became the norm because that is when many traditional pensions and Social Security began paying full benefits. But today there's nothing special about age 65.

People don't automatically begin thinking differently or experience a change in their abilities at that age; I'd argue that retirement should begin when you are psychologically and financially ready. If you follow a social norm or an expectation, you might end up missing out on great experiences that you'd love. Enter retirement when you reach the right *stage*, not the "right" age.

Myth 8: Retirement Planning Is a Financial Exercise

To retire well, you need a certain number of financial resources. That number varies from individual to individual, so it's important to make meaningful financial plans. However, your goal in retirement is to be happy *and* secure. This is something I believe in strongly. Research has shown that having more money does not result in happiness after a person achieves a living wage (between $60,000 and $95,000).[11]

Some retirees are buying land in Nevada and Arizona and putting tiny homes, RVs, cabins, or even converted vans on their property. They know what they want — a minimalist lifestyle that allows them to travel to see grandchildren and friends, or to host other RVers and campers on their land. They're happy because they know what makes them happy — and it's not a big bank account balance.

They're proof, along with strong research that proves the same, that happiness also comes from our social relationships, a sense of purpose, and psychological successes.[12]

Still other retirees find happiness in leaving a personal legacy, helping others, or saving the planet. While many volunteer organizations are looking for young people who want to volunteer around the world, Projects Abroad wants people 50 and over. The organization says they see many volunteers who want a career break or a meaningful way to spend retirement. They have projects that connect senior volunteers with the same priorities.[13] Networking and volunteering often lead to more opportunities and even second careers.

I also advocate for retirement planning to be more holistic and include the development of solid social networks and resources that will lead to, frankly, what I would say is a richer, more rewarding life.

Myth 9: It's Easy to Retire from a Career or Profession

Transitioning from a rewarding career can be challenging, especially if your personal identity is tied to your work.[14] Being a community leader, physician, teacher, etc. doesn't just define your vocation. For many people, work defines who you are. Because of such deep association, besides financial benefits, work provides meaning, a sense of purpose, and socialization with friends and colleagues.

Such benefits and identity can be difficult to replace, and to do so often takes time. Some retirees are satisfied with leaving their work environments completely, especially if the environments contribute to high levels of stress and anxiety. However, for others, disconnecting from one's work ethic may present a conundrum, and they may need alternative forms of work to adjust. But late stage careers may not be easy to find, especially ones that allow you to have flexibility and enjoy some leisure in retirement. To secure your desired new career, you may have to design and propose it to an employer.

Todd and his wife Traci both worked in the food industry. Todd managed the dining room of a five-star resort. His wife had her own catering business. Both were extroverts who enjoyed networking and socializing with their clients and customers. They also loved to travel, and both regretted the time their work took away from their exploring.

The 100-hour work weeks during their busy seasons were demanding, stressful, and draining. Neither wanted to give up their jobs, but they knew they were getting too old to maintain the pace required by their work. After going on a short three-day vacation to reevaluate their options, they enjoyed a delicious lunch on the beach at a food truck.

"I thought all these trucks served were tacos and hamburgers," Todd said. "This food was as good as anything the resort serves, and less expensive!" As they ate their gourmet meal and watched the crowds of customers at the truck, they were both struck by the possibility of creating a new experience—a food truck restaurant they could literally take on the road. They bought an Airstream, a food truck, and are currently designing a new life that combines the best of all they love to do—travel and feed people along the way.

Myth 10: We Only Have to Plan for Ourselves in Retirement

Julie describes her life as "being a sandwich." She feels trapped between taking care of her two children, both out of college, but living at home and unable to "launch" their own lives, and her parents. Her parents are too self-sufficient for a nursing home but refuse to move into a retirement community.

"I know I just need to let them figure it out and take care of myself," she said. "We're all functioning adults here. I just can't seem to let go and leave. I'm afraid by the time they figure it out I'll need help and no one will be there for me."

Just as we are living longer, so are our parents and older loved ones. Although past retirees had shorter lifespans, they could enjoy personal freedom in retirement. Many

21st-century retirees may have their retirement lifestyles altered to care for older loved ones, or to raise unexpected grandchildren, or care for adult children living at home. Yes, while we may laugh at the idea of adult children living at home after college or even instead of going to college, The PEW Research Center says that as of 2014, 33% of 25- to 29-year-olds were living at home with their parents or grandparents. Among a broader group of young adults, those ages 18 to 34, living with parents surpassed other living arrangements in 2014 for the first time in more than 130 years.[15]

So, Julie is not alone in being a "sandwiched caregiver," taking care of both the generation ahead of and behind her. She has more choices than most, however.

According to an AARP survey, approximately 50% of caregivers have no choice in taking on the responsibility. 60% of caregivers have to make work accommodations, such as reducing hours or taking a leave. Many times, caregivers must also face exiting the workforce early to provide care. Such a decision may alter their retirement future, both financially and emotionally. Over 50% of caregivers have difficulty taking care of their households. It also challenges them to continue to save at the same rate.

Summary

The promise of this book is to give you insights, tips, things to think about and examples of people who have done very well and then let you find your way to the next step. To this end, the above myths and their realities provide strong evidence that exiting from work has gone from being routine to complex for 21st-century retirees.

Potential retirees now face the need to develop a strategy for success that must take into consideration the fact that they might live upwards of 20 years longer than they anticipated. This could dramatically limit your resources and result in a modest lifestyle where you can only afford basic necessities. Because your parent's generation didn't experience several of the above issues, you may be faced with developing a plan for success with limited points of reference for guidance.

Jean and her husband John were both 55, overweight, smokers, and sick. John developed prostate cancer and Jean found a lump on her breast within six months of each other. They were both highly motivated to lose weight, stop smoking, and get healthy. It took them three years, but they both attained their goal weight, stopped smoking and took up jogging. They switched to an all plant-based diet as well. The lump in Jean's breast wasn't cancerous, and John's prostate was easily brought into remission. Their doctor assured them that the life changes they made could easily help them live well into their 80s.

"That's nice to hear," John said. "We're expecting grandchildren over the next few years and we want to watch them grow up. We just don't want to do it from a homeless shelter." He laughed, but he said he was serious. Medical bills and a change in jobs as a result of moving to a rural area with cleaner air took a toll on their income and they both wondered if financially they'd make it to age 65 when they could collect social security.

Given better treatments for common things like dementia, Alzheimer's, heart attacks, and strokes, people are living longer, healthier lives. The real question is, where is the income for that extra life going to come from?

The good news is, there is hope! For those who awaken now to the potential that an extra 20 to 30 years of living can bring, there's time for you to make better, wiser decisions. Knowing you can have a significant amount of that time living a much more healthy lifestyle than your parents, you'll be able to grab that brass ring, that *life bonus* now being offered to you. Now, you could very well experience the best time of your life like never before.

In this book, I'll share with you the real rich options you can have, *if* you prepare appropriately. I will show you all the various pathways you can explore to *exit from work*. Most of all, these pathways will serve you well as the foundation to create a better personal strategy for living and thriving.

Three Action Takeaways

1. If you haven't already done so, in a journal (possibly titled "My Exit from Work Strategy") write down your ideal age for retirement. If you have a financial advisor, share this goal with her/him and come up with an investment/savings strategy for the remainder of the time you have prior to making your exit from work. Create a realistic monthly budget that will help you stay on target with those goals and stick to it.
2. Revisit the 10 Myths shared earlier in this chapter, and see which ones you may have bought into. Journal about why that happened, and how you can stay grounded in the here and now reality of planning wisely for your upcoming retirement. It's never too late or too early to start. The important thing is that you take action and responsibility NOW for your future.
3. If you know someone who has created a well-planned, comfortable retirement for themselves, set up a time to take them out for coffee or a meal. Pick their brain about what has worked the best for them, and if they're willing, ask them for any pertinent referrals/resources that can help you get on the retirement success track, too.

CHAPTER 2: WHAT IS WORK?

I recently overheard a conversation between a high school freshman named Liz and an adult counselor named Sam. Liz was saying that she wanted to be an engineer. However, the discussion quickly turned from a friendly exchange into an interrogation. Liz expressed an interest in engineering based on a video she had recently seen on the internet. But immediately upon sharing her dreams with Sam, the tone of the conversation changed. Although he admired her ambition, he started to barrage her with questions such as, "What type of engineer would you like to be? Where do you plan to study engineering? What company do you want to work for? Do you know how much engineers are paid? How do you know engineering is right for you?" As a school counselor his job was to ensure students had the tools and credentials they needed to make their dreams come true. But his enthusiasm and desire to help her was misinterpreted.

As he spoke, Liz's face flushed more and more red with anger, and with good reason. She had just entered high school. She had years to figure out a more deeply researched career path. Sam was well-intentioned with his questions and did not mean to scare her. In his mind, he was just challenging her to think more deeply about her career because his thinking (like most adults with meaningful responsibilities) was that work is serious business. His intense questioning, though, could easily discourage rather than inspire anyone of Liz's age. Sam questioned Liz not because he didn't believe in her ability to become an engineer, but because he also wanted her to be successful in all aspects of her life that included her career, home, family, community, etc. This is all to say that adults can be very intimidating to young people without realizing it, even if they are professionals tasked with helping young people as Sam was.

Work, or the thought of work, is an activity that often occupies most of our lifetimes. When we're children, as soon as we can understand what work is, adults begin asking what type of work we want to do when we grow up. Although it may start as a cute exercise to see how creative we are, or who and what we admire when we are young children, in our teen years the subject of work quickly turns more serious. Early on it's okay to name a wide range of careers from soccer player to astronaut, but as time goes by, people challenge us to justify our career choices, which turns this into a more stressful exercise. The freedom to imagine a life we love and to pursue what we love can all too easily take a backseat as our loved ones push their personal agenda for us. The future they envision may not always be in alignment with their children's hopes and dreams.

Today, parents are often so focused on the *appearance* of work, that they fail to realize that without passion for their career paths, children wind up in vocations that are more obligations than opportunities. Work matters to us for many reasons, the primary one being the financial benefits it provides and the sustainability of an income. After all, come on, kids! We all need money to pay our bills! Work has equaled survival since the beginning of time. Before currency and markets to trade in existed, people hunted, fished, and farmed for food. If they didn't take part in daily activities like hunting for food and shelter, they were likely to die of starvation or exposure to the elements. Tribal members who couldn't or wouldn't contribute threatened the health and security of the entire tribe. Therefore, adults had good reason to make their children understand the importance of daily, productive work. It meant survival for everyone including themselves.

When Tyler was only 17 years old his father died suddenly from a heart attack, leaving Tyler, his three siblings, and their mother to carry on alone. Tyler dropped his dreams of college and took a job as a plumber's apprentice while his mother went back to school to become a nurse. Between them they were able to provide a good life for the family, but Tyler hated plumbing. He wanted to join the military, but set his dreams of becoming an airline mechanic aside until his siblings were grown. He waited too long to join the service and became too old to pursue his dream.

He did eventually quit his job and did go back to a community college to become an automobile tech, but it wasn't the same.

"I was hoping to travel with the Air Force," he said. "I'm getting to do what I want, which is work with engines, but it's not the same."

Tyler fell into the trap of working for money to pay the bills. He felt responsible for his family and thought he was stepping up to do the right thing. Sometimes doing the right thing means doing what we love and figuring out the rest, rather than doing something we hate, and putting our dreams on hold.

Today work still means survival, but in a different way. Over time, we've become focused on work as a means to an end; what it can provide to sustain ourselves. This has become such a prominent viewpoint that we often find that we don't appreciate the total value of work. I contend that most of us have neither examined nor challenged the expansiveness of what work means or can mean to us. Michael Jordan, after winning six championships, still came to work (yes, playing is work!) as do Tom Brady and Warren Buffett. So *why* are they working?

Could it be that they have a desire that extends beyond financial goals? If so, what could that be? I propose that there is in every one of us the dormant, if not emerged, desire to expand, grow, and evolve into our better selves that we have the potential of creating. Strangely, it's often not until the end of our careers when we realize the additional benefits - often intrinsic ones - that were always there if we had only acted on them.

Sarah was one of the lucky ones. She was laid off from her corporate office job making six figures a year. She panicked, but took her severance pay and went on a month-long sailing cruise with her son Drew to "clear her head."

"I'd sailed since I was five years old," she said. "I loved it and was good at it, but I never thought of it as something I could do for a career." On her cruise she met several other women working on large sail boats and yachts and realized she could make more money in less time sailing than she had at her corporate job.

"I don't know," she laughed. "A light bulb just went off. I realized I could make in six weeks at sea what I made in two or three months as a Vice President, and I could do it while doing what I love most — sailing."

After a few years working for other boat companies she had enough skills and connections to start her own company. Her son Drew helped her and together they created a company that taught people the sailing, cooking, crew, and cleaning skills they needed to land high paying jobs on big yachts.

"It's not the biggest company, or the smallest," she said. "But it generates enough income that I could retire tomorrow and just sail until I'm 100." She didn't plan to take a non-traditional job, or start her own business, but life had other plans.

"I tell people not to panic when they get fired or laid off," she said. "I tell them to get happy and look for the window or door that's about to open for them!"

While Sara was lucky enough to be forced into her dream job, that's not how it works for the rest of us. It's often not until we come to the end of our traditional work lives that we see beyond our wants (e.g. to have a secure job, live in a nice home, afford yearly vacations, etc.) to our true needs — such as belonging to a group of like-minded peers, feeling valued or respected, feeling connected, doing what we love and have a passion for, taking pride in our work and personal lives, giving back to society, leaving a personal legacy, bettering the lives of others, or making a difference to our community, our industry, our world.

We also live in a society that highly values the *output* from work. Work produces things for us to consume, admire and hope to have one day. Often people believe that work success is all about the amount of *stuff* they can buy. But there's far more beyond the new car in our driveway every year or our recent home renovation to living a fulfilled, satisfied and happy life.

Janet has been living in a converted Sprinter Van for ten years. She travels around the United States meeting up with like-minded people in meetups, campgrounds, and conferences. She converted her van before it was the popular thing to do.

"I guess that makes me an old timer," she said. "But I knew early on that collecting stuff I had to dust, and sitting around waiting for my kids to come home for the holidays wasn't my thing. I wanted to travel, to see the country, and to meet new people, and I am. Yes. I go to the bathroom in a bucket, and sometimes I don't shower for days, but I'm happy."

In the 1950s and 1960s people bought RVs and traveled two weeks out the year, staying in campgrounds before returning back to work. Now people from age 18 to 80 are buying and converting vans, and even sleeping in their cars so they can go on a "great adventure."

They use the gig economy to make money, or draw on their savings, or work campground jobs along the way. Whatever they do, they say the satisfaction they get out of their unconventional lifestyle is worth the inconvenience and hassle.

They're proof that our focus on work to obtain income to purchase our own goods and services can prevent us from appreciating that it creates things we can value even more—joy, community, and lives worth living. Work, particularly when your bills are few and you're living in your van, or at a campground or being a cottage caretaker, also allows us to develop a craft or skill by which we may become uniquely known.

Wolfgang Albert lives with his craft. His hammers, nails, files, aprons, and pliers are neatly stowed away in the trunk of his Mercedes-Benz Vito van — his mobile workshop. At 46, Albert is a traveling farrier and blacksmith. He has more than 200 horses he shoes at regular intervals.

All he ever wanted to do was work with horses. At age 16 he started his horse training and for the last 25 years he's done exactly what he envisioned as a teen — work with horses.

Regardless of the level of sophistication of our role or our job, work helps us form our identity. Whatever type of work we do, it provides an environment for us to interact with others and to accomplish goals that may make us feel at our personal best.

Take my father, who had a 30-year career as a doorman in Chicago. He migrated to the city from the south in the 1940s. His dream was to become a physician, but his ambitions were cut short, first, when he was called to service in the Korean War and later, when he returned home, he had to care for my grandmother. Dad didn't view being a doorman as a glamorous job. In fact, he frequently told my brother and me that he "better not ever catch us working as doormen." Nonetheless, Dad learned how to find value in his work and took it seriously.

He encouraged us to finish college and pursue our dreams because he hadn't been able to do that himself. Although he did not enjoy working outdoors during Chicago's winters and extremely hot summers, or interacting with guests who were difficult or refused to tip, still, my father found meaning in his work. As a result, he taught us work ethics and values that I did not fully recognize when I was a kid. For example, Dad would say, "Work is your livelihood, and it should be taken seriously."

Dad believed that if he had to be a doorman, he would be the best doorman ever. I attended college a few blocks from the hotel where he worked, and on occasion I would visit him there between classes. It always amazed me that my father knew everyone in the neighborhood. Although he was not a C-suite executive by a long shot, he had a tremendous amount of social capital in the community and knew a lot of influential people. If there was a movie or commercial advertisement shot at the hotel, they often asked him to be in it. If there was an influential guest at the hotel, he was selected to be on the service team.

A Chicago newspaper even featured my father as one of Chicago's "Most Adorable Doormen." He felt strongly that there was a special deportment a doorman should have, and did his job with pride. He arrived at work early, kept his shoes shined, and even though it wasn't required, he always had his shirts professionally laundered. He often said it was a matter of pride and professionalism. Over his career, my father definitely stood out as being special.

Although he did not have the most glamorous job, he was glamorous in it. Everyone knew to go to Dad if they needed advice on restaurants, entertainment, and places to visit in Chicago. They could count on him to have their car at the door on time so they wouldn't be late for their next meeting. Looking back on it, I realize he was really acting many times as a concierge as well as a doorman, because he would connect guests with the right person to get things done in the neighborhood. My father's job title was *doorman*, but it was the expertise, love, admiration, and respect he created for himself in the role that ultimately defined who he was. For my Dad, work may not have paid well financially, but it was rewarding in other ways we typically don't consider. Although he needed to provide for his family, his work's greater value was the feelings of self-esteem and purpose it provided.

Our value of work varies based on who we are and what our needs are as individuals. According to work expert Dr. Al Gini, no one is neutral about the subject of work.[16] Gini says, "Work, food and sex are the most commonly shared behavioral traits of adult life. While the latter two are subject to aesthetic taste and availability, and therefore constitute a discretionary choice, work, for 95% of us, is an entirely non-discretionary matter." Everyone has an opinion about work, which comes from preparing for it, engaging in it, or watching others perform it.

Even if we don't want to work, we still have to work until we can afford to stop. If you are fortunate enough to inherit wealth and not have to work, you will have an opinion about the work done for you by others.

If you choose not to work and have no money, you'll join another culture — the homeless. You'll still have to work at something, be it panhandling, busking, or bartering, but it will be work if you want to do more than rely on handouts.

Work is the one thing we cannot separate from other aspects of our lives. What we do becomes who we are whether or not we recognize it. John, a longtime friend of mine, aspired to become an attorney. Our friendship spanned over high school, college, and graduate school, so I knew how much being a lawyer meant to him.

After being a corporate attorney for several years, he took a role in a different line of business for his company. Although nothing changed except his job title, he told me he felt different when he was no longer introduced as legal counsel in meetings. Although his new role was a promotion and provided greater financial benefits, being known as an attorney was deeply personal to him. He still held a law degree and a license to practice law. He also had the ability to appear in court and provide counsel in certain circumstances, such as volunteer work.

The problem was that he tied his identity to *what* he was just as much as *who* he was. His work life couldn't be limited just to his office. It carried over to the role he played in society. Whether he was in the office, at church, or picking up his kids at school, everyone identified him as "the attorney" from his company.

In its most basic form, we can describe work as any activity we need or want to do in order to achieve the basic requirements of life or maintain a certain lifestyle. From a sociological perspective, work is anything that a person undertakes with a goal of being productive in a way that meets human needs. Work includes mental and/or physical exertion, but does not always have to include an exchange of money. For some individuals, work can be the fulfillment of duty or honor. Work and the way we perform it makes a statement about each person and their values such as whether they are trustworthy, reliable, and knowledgeable.

Why Is It Good to Work?

Regardless of how we feel about work, it teaches us great lessons that help us form and understand who we are. Even those who hate their jobs can discover that work provides an understanding of their likes and dislikes. Such an understanding can also catalyze a careful self-reflection that motivates us not only to change our job, but also may cause us to change the type of employer with whom we choose to work. In other words, this very negative work experience can change our lives quite dramatically for the better. It's the concept that one is "fired into success." This is a very real paradox.

Fired into Success

Fred Smith, the CEO of FedEx, recalled his Yale professor laughing at him when he first proposed his concept of a delivery service. "The concept is interesting and well-formed, but in order to earn better than a 'C', the idea must be feasible," his professor said. He might have been right. Two years into its existence, the company faced high fuel charges and a lot of debt.

Smith had $5,000 left and needed a miracle. Still believing in his concept, Smith took his $5,000 to Las Vegas and turned it into $27,000—enough money to cover expenses for one more week. In that same week he found another investor and now, his story is legend. Even though his approach might not be considered the smartest, for him, it proved to be the best.[17]

Ask Oprah Winfrey about failure. Her producer told her she was "unfit for journalism" and fired her. She found another job in Chicago where she went on to become the star and billionaire she is today.

J.K. Rowling, creator and author of the Harry Potter book series, was on welfare when she wrote her first book. Almost a dozen publishers rejected it before it was finally accepted. Rowling is a billionaire now, because she didn't give up.

Early in his career, comedian Jerry Seinfeld walked on stage, froze with fear, and was booed off the stage. He returned the next night and was able to deliver his routine. He could have let that one bad experience turn him away from his future, but he didn't.

Fired from the new television show *Frasier* after only three days of rehearsals, Lisa Kudrow said she was devastated. The next year she was hired to play Phoebe on the show *Friends*, one of the biggest sitcoms of all time. "If I hadn't been fired from *Frasier*," she explained later, "I'd have never been selected to be on *Friends*."

Henry Ford may have been a genius with automobiles, but he failed with investors. At first, he alienated his investors by taking too long to move forward. He lost funding twice with his delays and developed a miserable reputation in the auto industry, making it impossible to find funding—or so his investors thought. While Americans didn't believe in him or his idea, one foreign investor did and that's all it took to get him back in business.[18] Thankfully for Ford, that foreign investor wasn't afraid of a little risk. You know the saying: *The third time's the charm!*

There are hundreds of examples from all walks of life of ultimately successful people being fired, losing jobs, or getting admonished that their dreams weren't feasible at some point in their lives. The two things they all had in common were: they didn't believe what they were told, and they kept pursuing their dreams.

One of my favorite interviews about work was with a gentleman named Ron. Ron believed he wanted to be a doctor. Ron's parents didn't have the funds for college, so Ron had to put himself through on his own. He joined the Army Reserves, held part-time jobs and managed to pay for both college and medical school. His drive and determination to become a physician were great, but he was also influenced by his parents' strong desire for him to become a doctor.

During his time in school he started a painting business, and hired students who needed money. They completed projects on the weekends. After he started practicing medicine, he kept the business going by hiring a manager to run it. To his surprise, he later realized that being a physician was not as glamorous as he thought it would be. Often tired from working twelve-hour days, he didn't have the time he wanted to spend with his family. He also realized that getting paid for services from health insurance companies could be more difficult than getting paid by his painting clients. He had to treat several patients within an hour to make his hospital's business model work and therefore found he was not developing meaningful relationships with his patients like those that he was able to create with his painting clients.

After a few years, he stopped practicing medicine. Instead, he expanded his painting business to include residential and commercial clients. After several thousands of hours studying and tens of thousands of dollars spent on tuition, it was work, not school, that taught him who he was, what he wanted to be, and what values were most important to him.

Ron's career journey is certainly one to ponder when looking at how we might shift our concept of work and expand it to include its broader, more fulfilling aspects. Over our lifetimes, we will experience a variety of careers, jobs, institutions, and work environments based on our needs, values, and beliefs. What's important is not the job itself, but whether it brings us personal satisfaction . . . or misery.

A longitudinal study by the Bureau of Labor Statistics showed that baby boomers held an average of 11.9 jobs from ages 18 to 50. Common reasons individuals change jobs include:

- Higher pay
- Better benefits and perks
- Relocation to a different geographic area
- Career advancement
- Choosing a less stressful job
- Escaping an incompetent or negative boss
- Changing career focus
- Better work-life balance

- Reorganization at their company
- More interesting work
- Better work schedule
- Skills and abilities didn't fit the job
- Lack of recognition for accomplishments
- Company moved to a new location
- Better alignment between personal values and organizational priorities

Although all work may not be enjoyable, work can help us become better, even happier and more content people. Voltaire, famous for authoring the satirical novel *Candide* in the late 1700s, pointed out that "Work keeps at bay three great evils: boredom, vice, and need." Even the Bible says, "Those who won't work shouldn't eat." (II Thessalonians 3:10) These views of work as a "necessity" for living, are quite negative. Yet it's obvious that work is necessary, in most cases, to provide income and avoid poverty. As I mentioned earlier, our production of goods and services allows us to earn income and buy goods ourselves. Work also provides a daily structure that allows us to use time positively. Although we may dislike the routine tasks of work, it helps develop the discipline that can be transferable to many other parts of our lives. For example, we often hear people with a military background say that, "Being in the military helped me build the work ethic that has served me well in my new job as _____ (fill in the blank)."

Also, our work environments often come with policies and procedures we must follow which help us build and maintain ethical and legal standards. Although we may dislike being actors who must play the roles given by our clients, employers, or community, having our roles defined keeps us accountable. This accountability can help us build our reputation as being honorable, consistent, and dependable. Such associations can elevate our stature and motivate us to achieve greater goals. The lack of such associations can leave us lost, struggling to find our purpose, and give our lives meaning.

One joy of completely exiting from work is the amount of personal freedom that comes from not being confined to a structured workplace. However, the lack of boundaries and socialization can lead to unfavorable behavior. One-third of the U.S. population frequent commercial casinos, with more than half of those people aged 50 and older. In recent times, there has been an increase in the number of retirees addicted to gambling. Retirees often visit casinos to fill time and replace social interactions they once received from work. There are also studies that suggest an association between retirement and alcohol and drug addiction.

Amazing Senior Entertainers Who Continue to Inspire Us

Because the overall population is living longer, there are many older people who still enjoy being entertained. The entertainers themselves are also aging, but they are doing it with energy and enthusiasm. Who knew, right? Many still love doing what they do and plan to keep going with it for as long as they can. They often sell out performances because their audience still loves seeing them live and are happy to pay premium prices for the opportunity. I included this section to illustrate in another way how aging need not stop seniors from pursuing their dreams and talent.

Here are a couple of quotes from famous seniors who kept performing as long as possible:

"Musicians don't retire; they stop when there's no more music in them."
—Louis Armstrong

"Retirement at 65 is ridiculous. When I was 65 I still had pimples."
—George Burns

George Burns' show business career spanned over 93 years. He passed away in 1996 at the age of 100. He booked himself in Las Vegas and other venues that were clamoring for him right up until he was going to turn 100. George's logic? He said, "I can't possibly die before I hit 100, because I'm booked." The only thing that prevented him from making good on those bookings was an unfortunate fall in the tub in 1994. He never recovered from his resulting injuries, so those last few bookings had to be cancelled. But no one can deny he was the epitome of an entertainment superstar trooper.

Other senior performers still going strong include Carl Reiner (97); his best friend and early writing partner Mel Brooks is still booking Q & A sessions about his career with casino showcase audiences and other venues at age 93; Dick Van Dyke 94 has continued singing and dancing for many decades following his classic TV sitcom of the 1960s (created by Carl Reiner).

In 2018, Dick made a cameo in the film *Mary Poppins Returns* where he sang and danced his way into the hearts of a whole new generation, playing Mr. Dawes, Jr. (a descendant of his original role). His supporting role as Bert and his cameo as Mr. Dawes at the bank in the original 1964 *Mary Poppins* may have been something he never foresaw happening, but he was definitely up to the task!

There are scores of bands and musicians 65+ who can still rock out with the best of them and play to sold-out venues including The Rolling Stones, Diana Ross, Patti LaBelle, The Beach Boys, Ian Anderson (of Jethro Tull), Pat Benatar, Frankie Beverly & Maze, The Motels & Martha Davis, Gene Simmons (from Kiss), Bonnie Raitt, Eric

Clapton, various iterations of several Motown groups like The Temptations, The Four Tops and The Jacksons, Sting, Carly Simon, Paul Simon (he and Carly are NOT related, just in case you weren't aware), Carole King, Jackson Browne and many others. If you do some research on this, you'll be amazed by how many are still rockin' and rollin'.

Multi-talented friends of 32 years Martin Short (69) and Steven Martin (74) are still touring in their comedy show. They first met on the set of *¡Three Amigos!* in 1986 and their friendship has undoubtedly been filled with laughter just as they continue to create waves of it for their audiences. Never one to sit still for very long, Steve keeps cranking out albums that show off his still stellar banjo chops with the band The Steep Canyon Rangers. These often feature vocalist Evie Brickell—though only 53, she's been married to Paul Simon (77) for 27 years. They have three children together.

Some savvy TV executives are cashing in on the older audiences by writing material that revolves around older characters. New to CBS's 2019 fall lineup is the sitcom *Carol's Second Act* that stars Patricia Heaton (of *Everybody Loves Raymond* fame) as a 50-something former middle school science teacher who went back to school and got her M.D. The show has her cast as the oldest hospital intern and revolves around her struggles with her colleagues as well as her supervisor but it's clear that she has a natural knack with her patients.

Netflix's *Grace and Frankie*'s creator Marta Kauffman (*Friends, Veronica's Closet,* and more) cast two amazing senior actresses, Lily Tomlin (80 in 2019) and Jane Fonda (81 in 2019), to play "frenemies" who become housemates when their husbands come out of the closet about their decades long affair, divorce their wives, and marry each other. It's heading towards its finale in 2021 with the seventh season. It's been wildly popular among viewers of all age ranges. Veteran sitcom creator and producer Chuck Lorre (*Two and a Half Men, The Big Bang Theory, Mom,* and so many more) created *The Kominsky Method* for Netflix, starring Michael Douglas (75) as an actor who briefly had his moment in the sun many years ago, but is now a revered acting coach. His agent and friend is played by the amazing Alan Arkin (85).

This is just a smattering of the myriad professional, gifted performers who continue to live their dreams and entertain the world. If you doubt their numbers, just do a Google search on "Current Professional Entertainers over 60." The results will blow you away.

Why Work May Not Be Good

But there are times work *isn't* beneficial. Most of us have experienced a time when we have hated our job, or at least certain aspects of it. Maybe you didn't feel challenged or valued in your role, or perhaps you had a manager or coworkers you disliked. Perhaps you worked in a hostile environment. As mentioned earlier, work supports our livelihood, so sometimes the fear of not having a paycheck holds us hostage in negative environments for too long.

Although work can provide psychological success and positive well-being, working in stressful roles and a negative environment can detract from our well-being and negatively impact our health. Although my father was good at what he did, there were days he hated his job. Many of us have experienced times when we had to produce more with fewer resources, and to top it off, there was no appreciation for our hard work.

A few facts about working in America:

- The U.S. is the most overworked developed nation in the world.
- In 1960, only 20% of mothers worked. Today, 70% of American children live in households where all adults are employed.
- In the U.S., 85.8% of men and 66.5% of women work over 40 hours per week.
- Americans work 137 more hours per year than Japanese workers, 260 more hours per year than British workers, and 499 more hours per year than French workers.
- 52% of Americans do not use all of their vacation days.

Although work provides a great benefit to who and what we are, many of us hate work. This leads to the question, do we really hate work, or do we just hate being overworked?

There's a popular saying that goes, "Do something you love to do and you'll never work a day in your life." We all recognize the truth in the statement, but then so often say, "I wish I could make a living laying on the couch playing video games," or "I wish someone would pay me to hunt and fish and write about it." The fact is, we all know what we'd love to do forever if money and income were of no concern. The challenge is to figure out how to take what we love and turn it into something that can generate that income.

What if *we could* exit work as we know it and move into something that makes us feel empowered, valued, and successful? Work, or lack of work, *can* be on our terms - structured in a way that provides economic, social, and/or psychological value. So now, let's examine work and the transition from work in the 21st century, where we have a sufficiently long enough lifespan to achieve our own destiny. I'll show you how your current work can be leveraged to make the next stage of your life more enjoyable, rewarding, and successful.

Three Action Takeaways

1. Write down some of the hobbies and activities that you enjoyed in the past, even if these date back to childhood. Explore whether you still have an avid interest in any of these, or if there is some new interest in your current world that you believe you can be passionate about. Even if you're years away from your exit from work, keep considering these pastimes and possibly begin dabbling in them now from time to time. Doing so now will help you get a better grasp of what things you enjoy doing in your free time, and help you create a plan to work those into your retirement. Pre-planning can help avoid feeling lost and unfocused once you retire.

2. If you're already retired, or planning to within the next three to five years, what are some "side gigs" you would enjoy? Maybe it's consulting about your area of expertise while having the flexibility of setting your own hours and rates. Perhaps it's teaching or coaching. Start a list of the categories of work activities you'd like so that you can develop it as you roll along toward retirement. And if you're fortunate enough to have enough money set aside that you don't need or want to do any more work, consider

creating a list of volunteer activities you know you would enjoy.

3. Begin adding like-minded people to your circle of social activity, especially people with whom you don't work. Starting to widen your circle of influence while deepening and developing friendships ahead of retirement is just good common sense. It can pave the way for a smoother, fun and fulfilling exit from work.

CHAPTER 3: IS RETIREMENT BROKEN?

Many of us don't like to stay in any one job too long. Complacency with anything takes up valuable time that can better go towards finding the next great thing in your life. Overstaying can also minimize your positive legacy, leaving you with little or no time to earn it back. I'm sure you can think of several examples of when someone accepted the status quo and missed an opportunity to excel, or stayed too long and lost something of value.

I think back to a celebrated CEO. I'll call him Robert. In the 1990s, Robert drove his company's asset management business to award-winning growth. He was a good leader and well liked. The favorable economy at that time aided his efforts.

Although Robert had earned a great amount of money, he kept prolonging his retirement. He just couldn't let go. This was because Robert didn't take the time to reflect on the things that he especially appreciated about his current job, and then springboard from there into creating a plan to do something different–something challenging–something that would keep him motivated and continuing to grow. Instead, almost overnight the dot.com bubble burst.

The economy turned and fell into a recession. As a result, many of Robert's gains in his industry disappeared.

He became one of the first CEOs in the company's history to let go of employees. Not the legacy he wanted nor envisioned. Robert's story offers us an example of someone who was poised to leave, but because he didn't challenge himself to take the time to find his next great job, one that met his strengths and passions, he wound up staying too long. As a result, Robert missed the opportunity to have one of the greatest legacies in his company's history, and exited late, leaving behind one of its worst.

Andrew Luck, a very successful and young (only 29 years old) football player recently retired from playing quarterback for the Colts. Even though he was just 29, Luck said that the never-ending cycle of injuries, rehab, and then more injuries led to his decision to retire after 86 regular-season games. According to sportswriter Bryan DeArdo, Luck didn't miss a game his first three years. The next year wasn't so easy. He missed nine games in 2015 after sustaining an injured shoulder, a lacerated kidney, and a partially torn abdominal muscle. After playing in pain throughout the 2016 season, he missed the entire 2017 due to multiple surgeries to repair his injured shoulder.

Life got better for Luck. He returned to the playing field in 2018, creating one of his most productive seasons ever. He not only guided the Colts to the second round of the playoffs, he was also named the NFL's Comeback Player of the Year. Then injuries caught up with him in the offseason, prompting him to honor a promise he made to himself in 2016: that he would not go through another season of unknowns regarding his injuries and playing status. At a press conference he told reporters and teammates, "I haven't been able to live the life I want to live. It's taken the joy out of this game... the only way forward for me is to remove myself from football."[19]

What impressed me most about Luck was that at his young age he had taken the time to think about what he wanted, what his deal-breaker(s) for leaving football would be, and making a promise to himself to do whatever it took to ensure his happiness over his financial fortunes. He knew what he wanted, and what it would take to make him happy, even if it meant leaving the game he loved and had devoted himself to for his entire life. Unlike many players in the NFL, he had an exit strategy.

According to Draftmetrics.com, "49% of professional football players will be out of the NFL within five years. Of those players, 75% will have lost, spent, or squandered all the money they made playing football within five years or less of leaving the league. And for those fortunate enough to play longer, 75% of them will also have nothing to show for it within five years of their last season. The majority will get divorced, drink too much, and suffer from several football-related physical ailments."

Put another way, one of the biggest issues retired football players face is going broke. Going broke leads to other issues which can culminate in embarrassment, depression and then potentially to substance abuse, excessive drinking, and sometimes even suicide.[20]

Could being unprepared or having no exit plan happen to you? That could be the result if you get too busy to take the time to prepare prior to the changing landscape in your company. If you love what you do and approach each day with a high level of energy and passion, then you *should* stay. However, if you are ready to leave or even have it on your radar for the next year or two, don't stay just because you can't think of anything else to do. Take time, even if it's just 10 minutes every morning, to focus on what currently matters to you. Remember, you are not the same person you were when you started at your current workplace. I will address steps that others have taken to either stay or transition to another job.

Society has set an expectation that you should exit from work in your 60s. Most people hold on to this notion because that is when they see others leave, or it is when they qualify for certain benefits such as Social Security and Medicare. This leads to the question, *when is the right time for you to "exit work"?* The answer is - when it is right for you! Also, what does e*xiting from* work mean? Should you fully retire? Work exit doesn't have to be a complete disconnection from what you love.

Betty White still makes appearances in her mid-90s; Sister Jean is a 100-year-old icon as chaplain for the Loyola University Men's Basketball team; Samuel L. Jackson just starred in an action film at age 70. Things have changed and 60 is now the new 40—it is *middle age*. So, how did we arrive at the belief that we have to exit work at a certain age? To answer this question, let's look at the history of retirement.

The History of Retirement

The mention of a person entering their 60s can easily trigger a conversation about retirement. Somehow, we're conditioned to think retirement is part of a life course where certain activities and behaviors are appropriate for youth, middle age, and old age. This isn't true any longer. It used to be the case, but now you can research and discover that even during the times when that was the norm, some people did things out of sequence (like Grandma Moses, Dame Judi Dench, Colonel Sanders, and many more). In current times, that's more prevalent. It's not uncommon for 70-year-olds to graduate from college (I had a classmate in my doctoral program in his 70s). There were some savvy 40-somethings who retired from dotcom companies just before they crashed. We see more couples getting married in their 50s, 60s, 70s, and older.

There is no question life sequences are dramatically changing. So, what does this mean? With life expectancies approaching age 90, today 60-year-olds are closer to middle age than old age. Therefore, why should we assume any specific age be the "magic" *age of retirement?*

The Formation of Retirement in the U.S.

Historically, older Americans have thrived in the workplace. However, when and how they did that isn't commonly known. In early America, from 1700 to 1865, retirement was infrequent and designed to meet individual needs. Back then, landowners in their 60s deeded their property to their sons in exchange for a written agreement that stipulated the children would provide care for their parents for the rest of their lives. When life expectancy was 60 or under, the social norm was not to force the elderly into retirement. During these years, approximately 70% of men over age 60 remained employed until the Civil War.

For example, Benjamin Franklin was in his 80s when he served as the oldest delegate at the Constitutional Convention in 1787.[21] Although older workers may have had some limitations, there were benefits to working into one's later years, as previously mentioned. Wisdom and experience were valued in the workplace during our country's formation. Also, work environments were less structured and formalized. Organizations were smaller and allowed the customization of jobs to meet the needs of aging workers. This resulted in a win-win as employers retained the experience and wisdom of their older workers, and employees could negotiate a workday where they could contribute on their own terms.

But towards the end of the 1800s, work became more industrialized and the perception of older workers began to change. There was a cultural shift of power from elderly elites to the younger generation who viewed older people as impediments to progress. The participation of older people in the workplace was high in the late 1800s, but gradually began to fall, eventually resulting in higher retirement numbers. Older people began to retire for a few reasons: negotiated benefits, mandatory retirement rules, and new ideals about retirement.

Soon labor unions began negotiating retirement benefits in the late 1800s. The Baltimore and Ohio Railroad pensions were among the first created in 1884. Although many now believe pensions were created to be a generous reward from employers to employees for years of loyalty and service, this was not the intention with which they were designed.

As industries formed, work became more standardized and uniform. Flexible jobs that favored older workers gave way to specialized roles that required skill, speed, and precision, such as assembly lines. Emphasis then shifted to more scientific management styles. Efficiency experts became commonplace in many industries, carrying clipboards and stopwatches, constantly evaluating productivity and efficiency. As you would guess, this model was less favorable to older workers and even stereotyped them as being limited and less valuable. Because of this new workforce model, management in these workplaces started to believe that their workers had a fixed shelf life, especially those who performed heavy manual labor daily. Many felt that a 10-hour-per-day, 6-days-a-week lifestyle could only last for a certain number of years.

Management favored younger workers who they believed would keep production at a high pace. Another factor in their paradigm shift was that older workers with seniority were more expensive. However, organized labor unions wanted seniority rewarded and therefore favored older workers. They also wanted to protect older workers from being let go due to age discrimination. As business competition increased, management began to lose workers to competitors paying higher wages. The creation of pension plans was a compromise between management trying to keep younger employees and labor unions who were trying to protect and provide for older workers. Management agreed to make pension payments when workers hit their mid-60s because back then, many people didn't live far beyond that age.

Although pension systems provided an incentive for older workers to exit the workforce, early payments were not enough to maintain a retiree's standard of living. Then in late October 1929, the Great Depression began, causing the rapid elimination of many jobs, drastically reducing the size of the workforce. Around that same time, waves of new immigrants arriving daily created a new pool of younger, cheaper labor of which management was all too happy to take advantage. By the 1930s, 40% of older Americans were in poverty, creating a national crisis. In 1935, the United States created the Social Security system to address the widespread issue of destitution among the elderly, and it was signed into law by Franklin D. Roosevelt. Social Security emerged in response to great political pressure placed on lawmakers to relieve aging people suffering from poverty.

A few years later in the 1940s, the federal government provided tax incentives to employers who contributed to pension plans. Even though pensions and Social Security provided needed benefits people developed a negative perception about retirement because they strongly associated it with poverty. The phrase of someone being "on the dole" if they were receiving government money began popping up in the U.S. around this time. It originated in Great Britain around 1919. Because retirement plans provided benefits starting at age 65, and many institutions had mandatory retirement-age policies, there was also a societal expectation for people to exit the workforce in their 60s.

The Modern View of Retirement

At the turn of the 20th century, most people were about 76 years old when they stopped working. By 2010, the average age for retirement was 64. The retirement age has continued to fall as people in certain income brackets realize they don't have to continue to work, and financial reasons continue to drive why most people do or don't retire.[22]

Retirement advanced from 1965 to 1980 becoming more of an institution. During this time, legislation passed that improved Social Security and pension benefits. These laws ended mandatory retirement in the U.S. before age 70. They established Medicare to provide health insurance for seniors. Also, at this time, the Employee Retirement Income Security Act or ERISA, was passed to establish standards to protect the pension income of workers and retirees.

In the 1970s and 1980s, retirement became more associated with a lifestyle. The global recession during this period resulted in many employers offering early retirement packages to employees. This occurred at the same time people began living longer because of improvements in lifestyle and healthcare. What was originally intended as an incentive for more expensive workers to exit the workforce and create lower costs resulted in an obligation to make annuity payments and the provision of other benefits for much longer than projected. Retirees were now young and healthy enough to relax, travel and enjoy life with the benefit of guaranteed lifetime income. As a result, retirement became a destination for workers, and a growing liability for employers who eventually struggled to fund plans they never dreamed would become so generous.

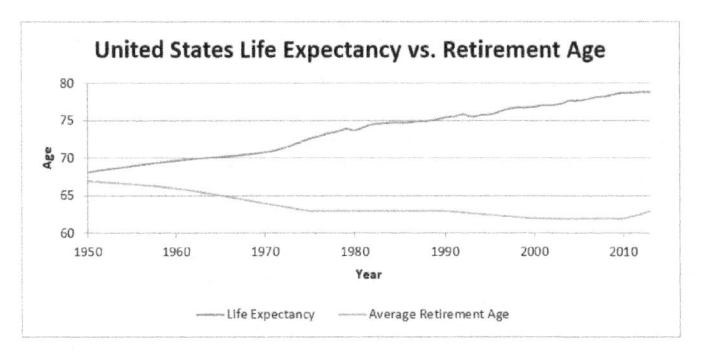

United States Life Expectancy vs. Retirement Age

Life expectancy data – Center for Disease Control
Retirement age data – U.S. Bureau of Labor Statistics

As shown in the chart above, in the 1950s the average American's retirement was in their late 60s and their life expectancy was the same.[23] By the 1990s their average retirement age was in their early 60s and their life expectancy was in their mid-70s. The guarantee of lifetime income, especially in retirement plans that guaranteed annual income increases based on inflation, became unsustainable.

In 1984, the number of active participants in employer-sponsored pension plans peaked at 30.1 million and declined to 23.0 million by 1998[24]. In 2015, only 20% of Fortune 500 companies offered defined benefits versus 59% in 1998.[25]

For many of us, our understanding of retirement is only the lifestyle we witnessed our parents and grandparents experiencing. Those lifestyles occurred during a more modern age of retirement, which began with great financial resources and just enough time to check off items on their bucket list before they were too old or passed away. Many of them had more than their share of hard physical labor and were literally feeling exhausted or tired, as the word *retired* suggests. Living their last days in a rocking chair, playing golf or sailing on unlimited cruises were rewards they were trying to capture before it was too late.

We remember when their lifestyles were the norm. However, what we don't realize is that they were living in a time that was not normal. What I mean by this is that when we examine retirement over a longer period, the expectation was for people to engage in meaningful and productive activities for as long as they physically, emotionally and mentally could. This doesn't mean that during a person's work life, leisure was unappreciated or perceived only as something one eventually engaged in on a full-time basis. However, there was more flexibility during that era to design a work-life balance that best fit the needs of the individual.

In 2017, *USA Today* reported the island of Sardinia, Italy as having one of the highest percentages of residents in the world that live beyond age 90. Several residents have lived vibrant lifestyles beyond age 100. People in their community attribute their longevity to staying active and practicing a healthy diet, while some maintain genetics plays a large part. Members of the community garden and live off the land. They also engage in as little or as much daily work as they enjoy, whether in the gardens, preparing food or doing other activities. It's their work and the pleasurable social interaction it creates that is also beneficial to their well-being.[26]

So, where are we now? What is our new normal? Now that we have entered the 21st century, many people have uncertainty regarding their life phase, which I call the *exit from work*. There has been an expectation of financial stability and leisure set by those who came before us. However, as I mentioned in the retirement myths in Chapter 1, several of those guarantees no longer exit. This leaves many of us feeling we have failed to achieve something others have accomplished. We had no cause to despair or feel like we have missed the mark somehow. Those that marched into the ranks of the retired before us benefited from an unexpected chain of events, policies, and even miscalculations that allowed them to have an atypical retirement compared to the norm.

Now is the time to embrace something different, which I believe can be even better. But we need to prepare. We must figure out how to create and build this better, new path for the years ahead. It's about designing a new vision for aging and then building the skills to attain those dreams you left buried somewhere in your past. It's now time to excavate them and reexamine them. But first, you need to figure out who and where you are regarding *exiting from work*.

Three Action Takeaways

1) If you are still working but have your exit from work on your radar in the next one to three years, give this a try. If you really love what you do there, and feel excited about going to work each day, take at least 10 minutes each morning to get centered, and take stock of what you're most passionate about at work. Write down any epiphanies you come up with. You may be surprised that your passion for work has shifted considerably since you signed on with your present employer. If so, that's fine! You have changed in a number of ways as you've been there.

By taking note of the things you currently enjoy the most about your work, you are planting some mental and emotional seeds to help you find ways to replicate those feelings once you make your exit. For example, is a key part of your enjoyment of work the camaraderie you have with coworkers? If so, what about your interaction with them makes it rewarding? It could be discussing books or films you recommend to one another; it could be exchanging family news. Wherever it falls on the spectrum, by defining what makes that experience meaningful and enjoyable, once you've identified it you can start planning retirement activities where you could create the same type of feelings. Remember, you don't have to wait until you make your full exit to begin cultivating new friendships or deepening existing ones.

2) If you know in your "heart of hearts" you will not want to make a full exit at the expected (or in some cases, company mandated) retirement age, brainstorm about new ways you could apply your experience in a different role there; possibly shifting to a part-time position that you would still find rewarding. The more clarity you begin getting now, the better your proposal to stay on in a different role and/or capacity will be. If there are any other people there who have successfully made such a transition, pick their brains a bit for some advice. If they've already walked the talk, they probably have valuable words of wisdom to share.

3) If you are married or in a committed relationship, if the two of you have not yet sat down together and openly discussed your plan for retirement, what assets each of you have to bring to the table to create the lifestyle you both want, schedule a time to go over these things, and the sooner the better. It's

never too early to begin planning trips and other fun activities you'll share during retirement; understanding your game plan regarding assets to make those events possible is a wise thing to do in advance. If you're single, you may want to sit down with a family member of member(s) to gain clarity for all concerned. If they know your wishes and your level of preparedness for your upcoming retirement, it can go a long way towards setting their minds at ease.

CHAPTER 4: WHAT DO YOU WANT EXIT FROM WORK TO BE FOR YOU?

As we learned in the last chapter there have been significant shifts over time in the structure of work and retirement in the U.S. We learned that in the pre-industrial age, a person's work life aligned more with their life span. During that time, employers restructured their employees' daily work to adjust to their aging bodies' capabilities. The workspace somewhat resembled the Italian island of Sardinia where elders were still very active, working in their community well into their twilight years. As a result, these elders remained involved in the daily work life of their island which also gave them more meaning and work life balance.

However, as the Industrial Age evolved, older workers were more and more devalued and displaced. Over time, retirement became something very negative, associated with old age and a lack of productivity. However, in contrast, in the second half of the 20th century, exiting from work became associated with a lifestyle of freedom, leisure and fun as the length of retirement increased, supported by pensions and other employee benefits.

It bears repeating that these additional benefits are not available to the masses. They are dwindling away as employers from several businesses are drastically cutting back the rich selection of benefits offered in the past. This leads to the question, where are we regarding retirement? Is it positive? Negative? Is it something people look forward to or fear? What are people searching for from retirement? What is retirement success, and what do we need to achieve it? I was curious–*very* curious. The research study in the Preface that involved spending over 1,000 hours to get answers to these questions (from individuals age 50+ approaching retirement), resulted in various insights you'll find throughout this book.

Finding Number One

The initial thing that I noticed after receiving feedback from participants in my first study was that the word *retirement* still has a very negative connotation. Why? Mainly because many people associate retirement with old age. It also implies that somehow, you are automatically beset and besieged by many limitations both physical and mental. In fact, the very definition of the word sets up deep internal conflicts such as many potential retirees feel wiser, more alive, more empowered, more aware, and more able-bodied than at any point in their lives.

This "60 is the new 40" point of view has its contrarians who still link their age with limitations. This negative mindset triggers anxiety around things like age discrimination. Think about it. This is the stage where people may be at their best. They have the maturity and wisdom to know what they like and don't like. They are more confident and self-assured than at any other time in life. They have the benefit of life experience and historical knowledge to know how to get things done. They also have more time and freedom to pursue their passions, especially if they are empty nesters. However, if they feel marginalized, especially in the workforce, their positivity can easily fade. Here are a few things these people said when asked about retirement during the interviews I conducted:

"But here I am now in my late 50s, and I'm just getting started. I do not feel like I'm ebbing out. I feel like I'm the person I was when I was younger, who had ambitions and innate talents, but I just need a longer time to pull it all together."

"So, if I had my choice, I would finish off my career in this role, and that would probably mean until I am 67. I mean, I feel the same as I did when I was 40. I function the same as when I was 40. So why should I not continue to do something I enjoy? I am smart enough to realize that I will not have that choice where I work."

Without question, many people achieved their greatest wins later in life. Colonel Sanders created his Kentucky

Fried Chicken franchise at age 65. Frank McCourt, a Pulitzer Prize–winning author, took up writing at age 65. Celebrity Chef Julia Child wrote her first cookbook at age 50, and Ray Kroc bought and franchised McDonald's restaurants in his 50s. There are clear examples of how the second half of your life can be the best stage if you find and follow your purpose and passion.

It's no secret that some people just plain old *dislike* work. I call them "Door Dashers." Door Dashers are devotedly onboard with completely exiting the workforce and never looking back. They view that as a welcomed relief and have no desire to return.

Jim was a classic Door Dasher. He had gone into the family business at 22, right out of college. It wasn't a job he wanted, and one that made him miserable for his entire career. He did it because it was what his family expected of him. Every time he tried to pursue a different career, they shut him down. He remained in his job out of obligation, fear, and a misplaced sense of responsibility. When he turned 60, he immediately retired over the protests of his family that he should keep working until he was 65. "Our family has a history of deaths at age 68," he told them. "I deserve a few years of life doing what I want to do."

Coming from a different point of view, Elizabeth never wanted to work outside of the home. She wanted to have a family and take care of her home. Unfortunately, she married into a situation where her husband didn't make enough to afford her that option. They both had to work to make ends meet and to maintain the standard of living they both wanted. When it came time to either fight for her job or take an early retirement package during downsizing at her company, Elizabeth was the first in line to retire at age 48. "We had to tighten our belts, and forego some luxuries," she admitted. "But I've never been happier. I'd rather eat peanut butter sandwiches than steak every night if it means feeling this free and relaxed."

At age 30, Lynn's doctors diagnosed her with arthritis. That plus other health issues made going to work "a living hell," in her words. She was in pain 24 hours a day, seven days a week. She couldn't wait to retire. While her health issues made her miserable, they weren't enough to classify her as disabled enough to claim benefits or retire. When she was in a relatively serious car accident at age 42, she decided she'd had enough and opted to retire, anyway. She would make a go of trying to live on the settlement from her accident. She moved into a used RV and found an affordable enough campground, and now lives happier, and more pain-free and stress-free than when she was working full-time and had healthcare coverage.

These people and others like them prefer a retirement lifestyle of leisure, which may include activities with friends and family. They also have health and other issues that make working a living hell for them. There is nothing wrong with being a Door Dasher and hanging out in a rocking chair if you find it less stressful and can afford it financially. But not everyone wants to be a Door Dasher. Unfortunately, parts of society assume these are the limits of retirement. Still, several looked and found unique solutions that work well for them, and these days, many more are considering and happily creating other options.

Finding Number Two

Many people approaching retirement age don't view their friends as successful in retirement. They envy their friends' ability to have free time and not have to work a 50-hour week. Yet they often think their friends are not doing meaningful things that make a difference. They know that traveling, playing golf and other recreational activities are fun and that they, too, would like to engage in those more often. But as they are now looking at retirement as a 20- to 30-year timeframe and believe they will eventually get bored if they do not engage in activities that provide more purpose.

A full life of leisure was appropriate when retirees had less longevity. It seemed fitting that people write out a bucket list and focus on completing it before their time ran out. Now, most people facing retirement aren't concerned about running out of time. Instead, it's the opposite–they're worried about having too much time. After asking themselves the question, "Will I outlive my money?" they next ask, "What will I do with my time?" Not having an answer to the second question is just as frightening as having no answer to the first.

When thinking about future lifestyles, many people facing retirement are concerned about becoming "Followers." Followers exit the workforce because they believe it is what they're supposed to do when they reach a certain age. For them, exiting from work is a tradition, not something born of desire. They have not taken the time to figure out what they want. In fact, they may feel they are being sentenced to their final stage of life. Followers engage in activities that fill their day but are usually unfulfilling. Here is what a few people had to say when we discussed their view of retirement:

"I want to do stuff. I've watched my friends. My stay-at-home friends and some that recently retired are all busy, but they have done stupid stuff. I will not join the bowling league and the clubs. I need more meaningful stuff to do and I haven't found that yet."

"I think anybody who thinks about this in-depth has to consider the retired people they know. We were just talking about a mutual friend who lives in Tucson and - what does he do? He plays golf, eats and drinks. What kind of life is that, really?"

I find it fascinating that many people share a deep desire to be Thrivers. When they exit work, Thrivers seek opportunities to grow and enrich themselves and others. They are in pursuit of their best life. They are also not afraid to take calculated risks with new challenges so long as they are fun, meaningful and provide psychological success. Here's what a Thriver I interviewed had to say about retirement:

"Retirement to me denotes end of life. It means no longer challenging oneself, no longer striving to contribute, no longer learning. Retirement means the opposite of taking risks, learning and growing. But those are the things I'm looking for. I want to take risks, I want to learn and I want to keep developing. And retirement is putting yourself in a very safe, stable, slow-lane environment where you don't get any of that stuff."

Thrivers are also looking for ways to redesign their work to create work-life balance on their terms. They do not have to take on a new career. However, they must have activities they find meaningful that provide personal satisfaction such as mentoring or tutoring. Initially, they may want to hold on to aspects of their work identity because work provides a sense of purpose and accomplishment. They enjoy socialization, friendships and associations. Thrivers are also looking for ways to convert their work into meaningful play, choosing when and how long they will take part in it. They differ from Followers because they seek fulfilling, enjoyable activities instead of settling for routine activities that just fill their day.

Dr. Dan, a pediatrician, sold his medical practice and joined Doctors without Borders, taking his skills and passion for helping the less fortunate to third world countries.

Thousands of men and women jump at the chance to volunteer around the world, often paying anywhere from $2,000 to $10,000 for the opportunity to do so. Why? Their desire to leave the world a better place than it is now is burning so brightly within them and they cannot ignore it.

Thrivers find ways to maintain parts of their work identity that allow them to have purpose on their own terms. Creating another career may not be necessary for everyone. What is most important is finding something that you find rewarding to do every day rather than merely filling your day with activities to pass time.

Finding Number Three

Many people struggle with the decision to exit work. Exiting work in times past was primarily viewed as an economic choice. Many believed if a person could afford to exit work, they would. You will see examples of this in retirement commercials that solely focus on how much money you need to retire, as if money should be your only consideration in making that decision.

Everyone with whom I discussed retirement in my study could actually financially afford a full exit from their respective workplaces. However, many of them lacked the confidence to transition. The reason some people struggle with the decision is that over the years, they have grown accustomed to allowing their work identity to supersede their personal identity, and often their worth. They've never envisioned themselves doing anything outside of those predictable work parameters. Naturally, they may occasionally permit themselves to envision a holiday vacation or having a day off where they don't have to think about anything. But the identities that others see them as, say, the doctor, the lawyer, the corporate executive, or the journalist at the newspaper bind them tightly. It's scary to step outside of that role and try a new adventure.

Work identity can come in three different ways: 1) They tie it to a profession such as medicine or teaching; 2) They tie it to a certain role or responsibility, such as being a manager or a leader in the community; or 3) They tie it (tightly) to the organization with whom they work.

Here's an example of # 3. You could be an employee in any corporation such as Nike, Salesforce or Google. You are so proud of that company's brand and what it represents that once you leave that organization, regardless if you held the Number 1 seat or the last seat in the organization, that break from your identity is extremely difficult. The thought of ever leaving that identity is similar to a baby bird learning how to fly, leaving the nest. It needs to happen, but someone may need to push you out of the nest for you to get it. The confidence necessary to do it on your own and do it successfully may be lacking. Most people are uncertain how they will replace their status as leaders, experts, or any other significant title they held.

Another barrier to having confidence about a transition is if your work environment was where most of your socialization took place. If you gave yourself to your work, and that's also where you formed most of your friendships, you're likely worried if those connections and interactions will remain after your exit.

I think back to a story about a colleague who became ill. Some days she was too sick to come to work. The organization could not insist that she leave, and they also didn't want her to leave because she was an exceptional employee. She was known as a leader and solid contributor in the business. Yet, it got to a point where her work became too draining on her physically. After one of our heart-to-heart conversations, I learned that her parents had passed, and she had no other family. She wasn't in denial about realizing she was too sick to continue to function at work. Rather, she was afraid that her "work family," which is what she called her colleagues, would no longer connect or even care about her if she retired early. She also didn't know how to replace the feelings of accomplishment and success that came from her role at work.

Finding Number Four

Many people lack the confidence to exit from work because they have no guidance to help them assess the many considerations involved in late-stage career transitions. Results from my study showed that most of the participants had a formal or informal career mentor to provide guidance during their career transitions. Many of these mentors also helped them network into better jobs.

However, when it came time to make the "retirement decision," their mentors (ten or more years their senior), were now completely out of the picture because *they* had retired. There is no question, retirement can be very scary, not only because you do it alone, but it is the only career transition decision that you will have to make that is likely irreversible. People retiring face many fears - age discrimination, and a real biggie (whether real or imagined) is *If I get this wrong, I'm stuck.* They will no longer have an advocate like that mentor inside the organization to take them back. They dread feeling like a rudderless ship with no direction.

To further compound this difficult transition, none of us know just how long we will live, yet we still continuously face decisions and must plan for multiple opportunities... and threats (e.g. health, etc.), that will present themselves.

So, this Wild West time in our history brings us to consider solutions that optimize our full potential while still keeping us safe, especially from financial risk.

What Are People Looking For?

My research findings show that people want something better in these extra decades of life, which is the gift most of us now potentially possess. Therefore, they won't be exiting from their current work lives in any way similar to the way their parents or grandparents retired. There is also no one roadmap to exiting from work in this world of many options.

Choices? You bet! Why not take a year off to go see the world? Or you might attend all your favorite musicals that you've wanted to go to for years. Maybe you just want to spend hours with your grandchildren, family, and friends. You might say, "Hey, if I have a 20 to 30-year life bonus, what's the big rush? I need to define who I am versus trying to do as many activities as I can cram into a day."

That may be very challenging if you've never witnessed someone going through the exercise of redefining themselves at a later stage of life. Certain people lean one direction, others in the opposite, and there are all manner of degrees in between. It is far from a "one-size-fits-all" scenario. All I'm suggesting is that complete leisure isn't on everyone's list, either. There is more complexity to a late-stage work exit, and therefore people have to figure out which options are best for them and create new models for those options.

What I discovered is that when exiting from their current work, most people are looking for a more holistic work-life balance and revisiting what work means to them. They crave being able to keep the best aspects of their work lives while moving forward creating a new work-living experience. This comes complete with incorporating into that mix as many of your passions as possible.

So rather than retire, perhaps 20 years early you now have many new and truly better options. Let's explore them.

Three Action Takeaways

1) Take at least 30 minutes to thoughtfully consider how much of your personal identity is tied to your career. Whether you've already retired or are approaching it sometime soon, please do this exercise. Then once you've discovered the ways your self-worth and other aspects of your identity are linked to your career path, journal about those. Leave some space underneath each item, and in that space list ways that you can create similar feelings of self-worth and satisfaction in new ways once you retire. Be sure to list what gifts you have to offer to others, as being of service to others always helps us recall our value. This is something many retirees don't take the time to examine and then may struggle with

for quite some time. Doing this exercise can help alleviate a lot of anxiousness and make your retirement flow much more smoothly.

2) Create a list of Top 5 activities or events you are looking forward to enjoying during retirement. If you come up with more than five, that's great! Don't look at this as a "Bucket List" so much as things you are excited by when you think about having the time and money to do them. Your list may shift as time goes by, so feel free to add to and edit is as you feel the need.

3) Decide whether you are currently more of a Follower, or a Thriver in your mentality about retirement. Give the portion of this chapter that addresses the differences a quick reread, if you like. If you have usually been a Follower most of your life, what are some ways you can shake things up positively, and take steps to becoming a Thriver? Journal about these, making sure to include how your life will be improved/enriched in your Thriverhood.

CHAPTER 5: RECLAIM YOUR LIFE

In prior chapters, we covered what work means and why it is so important. We looked at the history of work and retirement and how retirement evolved to what it is today. We also highlighted modern-day views of retirement. So where does all of this put you and your retirement dreams? You might still be undecided, with all kinds of thoughts flying all over the place. Why? Exiting from work, from that environment where you felt anchored for perhaps 30 years or more, is far from easy. As we've examined, that is because the very definition of work and retirement has changed from a simple model that fits most people to a more complex design that will be unique to you.

In this ever-changing work landscape, determining when and how to exit from work and what comes next can be difficult. Two things needed to increase your probability of success are:

1) Lifestyle activities that provide meaning and purpose
2) Meaningful social relationships

In this chapter, we will look at examples of how people accomplished the first item, and the following chapter will deal with the second.

Having It All

You can have it all when you exit from work—whatever that means to you. However, there are no formal systems that will figure out retirement for you and guarantee your income as in the past. Therefore, today you have to take charge of your future and design your own personal course. This may seem scary. However, the good news is, if you do it well, this stage of life, this Third Age,[27] can definitely be the best stage of your life. The diagram below is a pictorial representation of, first, what aging used to look like, and second, what it looks like today.

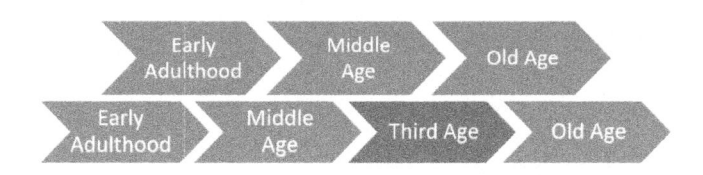

Early Adulthood > Middle Age > Old Age

Early Adulthood > Middle Age > Third Age > Old Age

In the past, people automatically transitioned from middle age to old age. They exited from work because they felt older and tired in their 60s. Life expectancy was shorter so people may have felt worn out and at the end of their lifespan. Modern lifespans are much longer, leaving many of us not only feeling we have much more to accomplish, but having the energy and resources to do more, too. We are capable physically and mentally to achieve these new, exciting goals. So, many of us are now craving for this *life bonus* of extra years. Instead of advancing from middle age to old age, there is now time for an uncharted new period referred to as the Third Age. Following are just some of many bonuses these up to 20+ years provide, helping to shape why the Third Age can be your best stage in life:

- You're wiser than you have ever been before.
- You may have more financial freedom than ever before, or at least networks of friends and new connections who can help you build a financial safety net, complete with an ongoing cash flow (so important for anyone at any age).
- Your life experiences have given you a better understanding of your likes and dislikes so you can more quickly choose jobs you enjoy versus taking on anything that feels like *work*. Remember this whole book is about *exiting from work!*
- You may have more personal freedom than at any other time in your life.

With this life bonus, you now get to experience extra years added onto your life, allowing you to do what is meaningful to you.

What Should You Do with Your Life Bonus?

In your early life, especially when you look at some societal expectations of people who came along in or around the baby boom era, there was an expectation—especially in certain families and communities—that you would aspire to certain jobs that had influence, benefits and stature. This meant following in your father's, mother's or even your grandparents' footsteps, carrying on in their same profession. It also may have meant pursuing a career someone picked for you.

Many people tried to live up to what family members or even friends thought they ought to do. More traditional views of work and taking on expected professions were pretty commonplace. For several American generations, many became professionals like doctors, lawyers, and teachers. We looked for approval from our parents based on us hitting certain objectives. It wasn't like what millennials experience today, where they're encouraged to explore more unique and broader career options. Many parents today also encourage their children to consider more creative jobs that allow them to explore nontraditional work experiences. We now consider entrepreneurship a strong option for a healthy, long-term career. It's okay to start a business out of your garage or turn a hobby like gaming into something that can be lucrative. These options are now becoming common.

Many of us became who others thought we ought to be—whether that was our parents, our teachers, coaches, clergy, and so on, or even careers that we saw on TV that seemed ideal and viewed as safe. I think back to growing up watching certain sitcoms and it just seems like those shows projected a certain family model. They encouraged everybody to aspire to be like the characters on *Family Ties* and or *The Cosby Show*. Eclipse that image with *Modern Family*, an era where you have a family composed of diverse dynamics that once weren't traditional.

In our current era, one thing people are seeking is something they may never have been able to reach in earlier decades - for the first time, doing what they are passionate about and ideally desire. Doing what we think we ought to do is our way of stepping up to certain responsibilities we face daily. This, though, is more about *working to avoid losing in life* versus working to win. We have opted for the former, preparing for responsibilities we think we will have in life.

Many of us knew in our teens or as new adults preparing for careers that one day, we would have families. We would then later have a house, and the progression then evolved to needing to pay for our children's education. The next logical step was planning for retirement. Taking the risk of joining a rock band wasn't something most of us were comfortable pursuing. So, if that was our dream, we probably pushed it aside in favor of the more secure route. It may not have been ideal satisfaction-wise, but it produced a very good career with a very good salary.

Now for the first time in our lives we don't have to worry about where we are going for financial support. Maybe you have created a nest egg. Some are small, some larger - but you have something that you can work with even if you decide not to complete an exit from work. You can reduce work or structure it to align with what you have so you can take a risk to do what you ideally desire. That's a great freedom, especially given the fact of your life bonus. Remember, "60 is the new 40" and we should take advantage of that.

There are plenty of examples where people now say that they have no more responsibility as it relates to a family—if that was a responsibility—or to supporting aging parents, paying a mortgage, etc. They are finally free to do what they feel is fun. They can use their imagination, they can take risks, they can be as creative as possible. They can create a new identity for themselves, or they can reinvent the identity from their work life, modifying it in personally gratifying ways.

One example of this is a company in Ohio called Bonne Bell Cosmetics.[28] As of the writing of this book, the company underwent some restructuring. Bonne Bell is a very interesting family-owned business. One day, the owner (in his 70s) came in to do some work and realized that they were outsourcing a lot of work to other companies. He realized that several older employees that no longer worked for the company still had their identity tied to the brand. They continued to love the work they had put in and held a steadfast belief in the product. There was a great loyalty among them for Bonne Bell's contribution to the industry; they had genuinely believed in what they were doing every day at work. The owner thought, *what if we created a division of this company just for those retirees to come back, and they could figure out how they wanted to work?*

These retirees had exited work, but an exit for them may have been more of a physical move, while psychologically their heart was still there. They missed the social environment that provided constant new friendships; they missed the accomplishments—completing tasks, fulfilling orders for new clients, going into new markets and growing the company. The lack of doing those activities left a hollow place in their lives.

The owner created a division that was only for retirees. They came in and took over assignments formerly outsourced. The average age on the assembly line was 72. The waiting list to come back to work was so long that they couldn't fill the demand for all of the shifts. The workers received no benefits but got paid to work four-hour shifts in their preferred time slots.

What occurred was a tremendous amount of productivity and a resurgence of enthusiasm inside the company. The owner's epiphany created the situation of retirees returning to work who were so much more efficient than in his previous business model that it became more affordable for him to discontinue outsourcing certain activities. This was an example of individuals reclaiming their lives. They didn't want to work if work was just a financial means to an end.

They no longer needed to work supporting their families or to pay for a car or house. They only wanted to do the things they enjoyed about their work. Picking their own four-hour shifts, redefining what type of work they wanted to do and honing in on the aspects of the job they enjoyed plus eliminating the parts they didn't, did wonders for the workers' enthusiasm. This resulted in greater productivity. By reclaiming their lives they proved you didn't own your life when you were just doing what you ought to do.

In your life, although you undoubtedly satisfied a lot of the conditions you were responsible for, it may not have ever been your life. It was probably very fulfilling for you, but you sacrificed to create security for your loved ones. They may have been your children or parents that you were caring for, maybe your nieces or nephews, or your community. Whatever the parameters, it was a life of servitude and sacrifice. That doesn't mean you didn't get personal enjoyment out of it. You may have gotten great satisfaction out of investing in others and watching them blossom.

Now it's time to reclaim your life. This is the opportunity to invest in you, to actually—for the first time—figure out what you want to do. There is always a gap between your actual self and who you feel you ought to be to fulfill a responsibility. People usually work toward who they think they ought to be, and research shows when you have a gap between that image and your core being, if you don't hit that goal, anxiety grows.[29] You didn't live up to what others wanted for you. However, a gap that exists between your actual self and who you ideally think you should be results in regret. In that case, you didn't live up to what you wanted for yourself.[30]

When people don't hit their target or close the gap between who others think they ought to be and who they really are, as time passes, they become less concerned about the target they missed, and may have some regret. It is not unusual to forget the target. However, individuals who don't hit the target or close the gap between their actual self and their idealized version of self experience much greater levels of regret.[31]

What I'm saying is this: Because we now have the gift of an extended life period wherein we can achieve those things we ideally would like to reach, things that provide us with fulfillment, feeling ready to leave this earth with as few regrets as possible, why not go for it?

Take Stan, a successful businessman and an accomplished scientist. For many years he worked in media services and from that, spun off and developed a prospering company. He never intended to retire.

One day, a company approached Stan with an offer to buy his company that he couldn't refuse. It was far more money than he thought the company would ever be worth. In fact, he had never thought about the actual value of the company, nor ever considered selling.

After the sale was complete, Stan wound up with a significant windfall. He was in his late 60s, and thought because society puts pressure on you to exit from work in your 60s, that was the thing to do. Because he had been so busy working hard for many years, he never really had time to reflect on what he thought his life should be. He hadn't considered what activities would make him feel fulfilled if he ever did something outside of work.

What it boiled down to was that he sold the company because everyone in his peer group was exiting from work into retirement, so it felt like he would be smart to follow suit. The prospect was even more appealing because someone wrote him a big enough check that he could make an economic argument to exit the industry. Because of these choices, Stan engaged in "Follower" behavior.

Six months after the sale, I got together with Stan and asked, "So, Stan, what are you going to do with all of this money?" He replied, "I haven't even thought about it. I don't need it for anything. I just know I need to buy another company because I really miss working every day. I'm bored out of my mind." I didn't think too much about this, but believed he might be going through a period of seller's remorse that's common in most major transactions. I figured he'd soon get over it.

Roll the clock forward another year and we meet again. I asked, "Hey, Stan! Are you having fun spending your money?" He sighed and said, "I really don't care how much money I made. I'm bored out of my mind. I've got to buy another company."

That stunned me more than a little. I said, "Well, don't you want to talk about all the things we planned for financially?" It became very clear to me he was confident he would be okay financially. His motivation in meeting with me was because he liked the social interaction and enjoyed our intellectual discussions on several topics. That reminded him of the daily interaction he used to get at work.

I thought eventually he would transition out of this. Flash forward six more months: I see Stan and he tells me about all these things he's doing. They are typical of what most retirees do, but I can tell they're just not a fit for him. Seemed like one of his biggest excursions was walking the dog every day. Our discussion ran the very narrow gamut of, "I walk the dog every day," to "I take the dog to the groomer a couple times a month." I began questioning why he was taking the dog to the groomer so often. It seemed to me they were going to the groomer because Stan needed to nurture, just like he had nurtured and mentored some of his employees. The dog was getting excessive amounts of attention and I imagined was becoming very exhausted in this process.

The happiest day was probably three months later when I met him. I looked at him, and he seemed lighter. His energy was much more upbeat. I said, "You look so much happier now." He answered, "Yes, a company asked me to be a consultant twice a week."

This is what I mean by "reclaiming your life." Stan was evolving from this place where he was feeling obligated to be who he thought he ought to be, because that's what you do when you hit 60. Now he was headed to a place where he was doing what he ideally wanted, following his bliss. He was becoming a Thriver. For Stan, that meant being engaged in business. His exit from work took him from the demanding task of being CEO of a company, responsible for things he didn't like at work and brought him full circle where he discovered the things he loved about work. It was somewhat psychological, but he never desired the full exit from work.

When we talk about an exit from work, we have to talk about what stage, what types of exits are important and what are the steps you need to go through in terms of an exit. In Stan's case, an immediate exit from work was, in many ways, detrimental to his well-being. A gradual exit from work was very much needed here. When Stan went back to the company he went from working two days a week to one day a week. Then, one day, he came to me and said, "I'm ready to be done with that altogether."

Stan now enjoys spending time at home. Being with his dog has replaced some of the satisfactions he used to get from work by doing things like mentoring younger people as they started their careers. He now is at a point where he doesn't want to commit to a schedule. But he still enjoys some aspects of being busy.

Maybe he takes on a project one summer, and maybe the next summer he doesn't. He gradually figured out what an exit from work means for him and found his ideal self. One of his favorite things is mentoring, coaching and helping people. I believe that will always be at the core of who he is. Now, to what extent he wants to do that may change. This may not be something he wants to commit to 80 hours a week, but he enjoys the engagement activity.

The other individual I think about when I talk about reclaiming your life is a gentleman I worked with when I first came into my career—Sam. When I entered banking in my 20s, Sam was approaching his 70s, if not already in his 70s then. He had worked beyond the period typical of the early 1990s workforce.

Sam and I got to work together in corporate and investment banking for a couple of years. I thought he was a fantastic banker with a very sharp mind. One day, he announced he was getting ready to retire.

One thing that I never noticed until I thought back on it and had some further conversations with him is that people were always asking Sam when he planned to retire. Whereas, some people thought, "Hey, we're engaging in a casual conversation, just a friendly exchange to develop some comradery," I don't think they had any sensitivity or even an understanding that Sam didn't want to engage in that conversation. He didn't enjoy it. It made him feel ostracized. The way he interpreted it was as if someone was asking, "Why don't you hurry up and leave?" Understandably, he resented that.

When Sam announced his retirement, I had never seen a celebration more elaborate. He had clients—some for over 30 years—that showed up to speak on his behalf, and even our CEO. His family was there. At 70, he was healthy with a great career that had rewarded him very well financially. He could go off into retirement and never worry about a thing for the rest of his days. His wife was healthy also, and they could do whatever they wanted, whenever.

After the celebration, I thought to myself, "Wow. That's the way I want to be celebrated at the end of my career." I remember to this day the exact words of his speech. He made two decisions that he knew were right in life, although he made a number of others where he had to wait to see if they were right. The first decision was to marry his wife. The second one was going to work for the company where he built his career for over 30 years.

It reminded me of a quote by Sigmund Freud that says there are two wellsprings of life that contribute to one's well-being. One is work and the other is love. To think Dr. Freud studied this from a scientific perspective and came up with that, while Sam, with seemingly no knowledge of Freud's quote, was able to point out that those were the very two things that energized him the most out of his life—that was rather interesting.

Three months later, I came to work early—about 7:30 in the morning—and Sam was sitting at his old desk. Shocked, I blurted out, "Sam, what are you doing here? You're retired." Here I was in my 20s, thinking I'd love to have all the freedom in the day to go on fun adventures. I was at a stage in my life where I was building toward who I *ought* to be. I *ought* to be a good professional; I *ought* to lay some footsteps to plan for a family. I *ought* to reach the point where I could afford to provide for the future. Therefore, I had to be there to work towards making all that happen. I was envious of him, sitting there, accomplished and over those hurdles.

He hadn't answered me, so I prodded again, "Sam, why are you here sitting at your desk?" He looked at me and said, "Gregg, I can't do it." I asked, "You can't do what?"

He said, "I can't retire. I'm lousy at it. I'm failing retirement." This was so unexpected it took me by surprise. This man couldn't fail anything, from my perspective. Trying to be empathetic, I asked, "What are you talking about? Well, why don't you go on vacation? Maybe go see your friends, or spend extra time with your grandchildren?" He shook his head, saying, "I've done those things. They don't complete my day. They're just taking up time. I somewhat enjoy it, but it's not like I was when I was at work."

Here he was in his 70s, had exited, and could not come back or couldn't figure out a way to come back. So the first thing he thought to do at 7:30 in the morning was to come and just sit at his desk because that gave him happiness and reminded him of things that provided him joy in the past.

He had exited out because he thought that's what he *ought* to do, but after being at home for a few months, he realized that he wasn't doing what he wanted to do. He still wanted to be a banker. A complete exit from work was not the right thing for him. He thought it would be because the stereotype was that you retire when you reach a certain age. Sam made the wrong move and was struggling to get his life back, but didn't know how.

Soon after that, he had an interaction with the CEO of our company. Everyone saw he was miserable, so the CEO arranged for him to get a job as a personal banker, opening checking accounts at a branch near his house. This may seem like a demeaning task for someone as senior in the organization as he was, but for Sam, this was wonderful. He was close to home; he got to interact with some of his old colleagues; he knew the customers that came in the door because many of them were his neighbors.

Some people looked at him strangely and said, "Why are you doing a job designed or intended for a young kid right out of high school? We know you don't need the money." For him, however, this was one of the happiest times of his life. Some of the retail clients that came in were executives who worked in companies in the area. They would come in at lunchtime and do their personal banking. Sam knew who they were because he had worked with them as a corporate banker.

There was one company that had stopped doing business with the bank for whatever reason. When the CEO came into Sam's branch to do personal banking, Sam asked about the company. He got wind of something that the company was doing—an acquisition or some spinoff deal—and he talked the CEO into accepting a proposal from his old buddies in corporate and investment banking. That turned out to be one of the top revenue-generating pieces of new business for the bank that year.

Because of this effort and suggestion, Sam reclaimed his life. He found what he ideally wanted to be. Maybe it had elements of who he *thought* he ought to be or *who people said* he ought to be. That was okay. The most important thing was he got to be in a position where he finished life without regrets. So Step 1 in getting your life back is: don't accept societal norms. Spend time figuring out what is right for you. Is it a complete exit? Is it a gradual exit? Is it no exit? Figure out what it is and go claim it. In Sam and Stan's cases modifying a career identity was associated with who they ideally wanted to be. However, it doesn't have to be. I have had people tell me they would like to play in a garage band, work as Disney characters at Magic Kingdom, or write mystery novels in their next stage of life. Do what works for you and avoid regrets. Finally, if you wind up feeling like you don't know, consider seeking a coach who can help you go through the options.

Moving from Money to Mission

This leads to the question: What is success? Success, especially in retirement in the Third Age—and many stages of life—is now being defined through purpose, meaning, and psychological goals more than ever before. The exit from money to mission is an acknowledgment that many people now have financial freedom at this stage. Maybe not full financial freedom, but definitely more than they've ever had before. Going to work every day is not so much about the money as it is them figuring out and getting comfortable with whom they are, and what they want to be at that next stage of life. Do they want to continue with the identity that they had for their professional/primary careers? Or do they want to transition from that somehow, keeping some elements of it and taking it to a new space?

For example, an individual may be an attorney at a large law firm and identify him/herself that way. They may be ready to stop the 80-hour week grind, meeting with clients and colleagues, mountains of research, going to court every day. But they like the psychological satisfaction that comes from being known as an attorney in their community and being respected as an authority in their field when they go to conferences or interact with peers. The struggle remains post-job in figuring out how they keep those aspects they enjoyed during their career while transitioning into a new identity.

It may be a transition to create a way to practice law on their own terms. Maybe working part time at a smaller firm might suit them. Another option could be to reduce the hours at their current firm. Perhaps doing something more civically inclined would be perfect for them, such as working at a legal aid clinic.

I remember an individual I spoke to during my research for this book. Anthony had a very successful career as a corporate attorney. He was very well-known throughout the city by high-ranking public officials, corporate executives, and community leaders for cutting deals that got national attention. In many law firms, there is a mandatory retirement age. It's often 65, and put in place for succession planning reasons - to give younger attorneys an opportunity to advance up the ladder. I'm sure there are other benefits to the firm by having limits around that, because they also want to ensure that their attorneys don't work beyond the period where they're competent to serve in the role. It's a way to make sure that people do not stay beyond the point where they could create a liability for the firm. What's that old saying? Outlive your usefulness?

I'm assuming that these mandatory age limits made sense back when life expectancy was shorter. But in today's current environment, the mandatory retirement age of 65 may be very limiting and unfair in myriad ways.

Anthony reached this mandatory retirement age, still at the height of his career. He went back to his firm and said, "Look, the evidence shows from my productivity that I've never been better at what I do. Can I have an extension?" Anthony got an extension for a few years and continued to work, continued to thrive, and continued to generate revenue. I think he received another extension after that. This continued until he reached his 70s, and he still wanted to continue. But the firm said no, that he'd reached his maximum.

Because he had devoted his life to his work, his family life suffered. He was divorced, and his adult children no longer needed him daily. He had wrapped his identity around his profession. He struggled to figure out other things to do to give him the satisfaction of completing tasks, of being known as good at something, setting goals for himself that the law provided and that his office provided. He also struggled socially because his friends were his work colleagues, along with people he knew in the industry when he went to conferences and engaged in political campaigns. Now he found himself removed from those circles.

Anthony tried to create a happy medium resolution. He went back to his firm and said, "I want to continue working. I know that I've reached the mandatory retirement age and you've extended me a few times and can no longer do that." They worked out an agreement where Anthony would go work for a nonprofit that the firm supported. The firm would contribute to a reduced salary for him. That wasn't an issue; Anthony had been very successful and no longer needed the money. In fact, he could have retired 10 years prior and most likely would not have outspent his money.

This provided Anthony an opportunity to continue operating within his established identity, which was of top importance to him. He wasn't ready to let it go. Thrilled to release the long work hours, he still held on to his network of friends. He could keep his social status in the community as an expert in his chosen field.

Anthony's story illustrates that retirement goes beyond the money. The mission becomes helping the community with the skills you've developed as a professional. It's an opportunity to give back to younger colleagues who need coaching to continue in the profession, or further the purpose of the work you view as important. Anthony's freedom to go this nonprofit route provided him the chance to coach young lawyers. It was chiefly about lifestyle tradeoffs. Some of those tradeoffs might be that you continue in the work you were doing full time before, but now it's not about the paycheck. It's about the satisfaction that you get from doing the work—especially when working with an organization you believe in, or when you are the owner of a company that does things that highly serve the community or promote your perception of the public good.

Going from money to mission also has a lot of meaning for individuals interested in securing their career legacy. They're invested in benefiting the next generation rather than leaving them in a place where they have no historical reference on how to do things. That's very important. The mission becomes the focus of developing an identity.

The move from money to mission is crucial. Many people don't know how to find that mission. Discovering the mission requires self-reflection, similar to when you were younger in life. In your early stages in life, from the time that you first began speaking, someone was probably asking, "What do you want to be when you grow up?" Then you get to school and your counselors ask you what you want to do, where you want to go to school and how you want to do it. It is very intentional in most cases where you end up in life, from a career perspective.

If we spend 15+ years training for our first career, why aren't we spending more time trying to figure out what our transition should be later in life when we try to exit from our primary careers? Without this reflection and thoughtfulness, people wind up in a space of unknowns and vulnerabilities.

Three Action Takeaways

1) Do you feel that there are parts of your life that need to be reclaimed? Things that you've put off or maybe even thrown away/released because you felt you'd never have time to do them? If so, write them down and know it's not too late to include them in your plans for retirement. Some of the parameters may have shifted a bit as you've grown older, there may be a few limitations you wouldn't have had 15 or 20 years ago; if so, think about some of the different ways you can still achieve those dreams/goals, or at least new ways that you can recreate the feelings that those things brought up for you when you first considered doing them. Write those down; create a game plan that you know you'll be happy executing when you make your exit and promise yourself to stick to that plan. This creates more energy and momentum around feeling good about your exit from work.

2) Read some books and/or articles about people who became successful late in life by doing things that they loved. Doing a quick Google search will provide you with plenty of great examples. Read a book about those people, or watch films based upon their lives. Doing this will help you find new inspiration and a reassurance that no matter our age, we can still contribute value to our communities, society and the world.

3) If it suits you, create your own Money to Mission Transition plan. Revisit that portion of this chapter for inspiration. Come up with a few solid steps you can take when dealing with that time in your career that will make the transition appealing and smooth.

CHAPTER 6: LADDERING BONDS AND BUDDIES

Candace is in her 60s. Until now she has had a very successful career as a speaker and trainer, earning six figures every year for the past 20 years. She has also been wise about saving money, but because of a nasty divorce she has less than $200,000 in savings put away for retirement. She also has little desire to retire but recently went through knee surgery that kept her from working.

However, Candace has something that many others don't - a vibrant network of people who have referred business to her over the years. Therefore, she has a pathway to change her current financial state. Is Candace lucky, or is something else going on here?

I would argue that Candace's success has been and will continue to result from her networking focus and consistent development of her network. But many people don't realize the significance of building a vibrant network isn't just about new career or business opportunities. Rather, it can also be about developing relationships—and even more so, friendships. I refer to these people as your "buddies." These are unique and utterly irreplaceable individuals there for you when you need them the most. In fact, for many who live alone today, buddies offer an extended family. For example, I know several people who have done this, and have read about thousands throughout the world who have turned their friends into *family*.

So, what's the commonality between *bonds* and buddies? When we think about retirement and how people traditionally planned for it, as pointed out in prior chapters, the biggest concern was whether you would have enough money to last for the rest of your lifetime. The second concern was, how healthy would you be in retirement? The answers to these questions offer some clues about how long you might live and therefore what financial safety net you should create.

In the past, there were a few usual ways people went about financially preparing for retirement. One was investing in bonds. I still use bonds as a meaningful part of an investment portfolio when I help people prepare for retirement. Although there are several other investment instruments available for an investment strategy, such as stocks and real estate, bonds often become a larger part of the investment mix as people age.

People like bonds because they are typically safe. A bond represents a loan to an entity—which may be a local municipality, the federal government or a corporation—

where that entity commits to repay you the amount borrowed plus a certain rate of interest income within a stated time period.

Bonds are often attractive because they create a source of steady income that usually can go toward paying your bills in retirement. They are often used to replace the consistent income you were used to from your job.

So, what do financial investment bonds have to do with your buddies? Maybe not much, at least on the surface. However, strategies used with financial bonds are cross-applicable to developing social bonds. Social bonds are the relationships you create with people that add value to your life such as friendship, fellowship and a sense of belonging. Those are the "gains" you receive on top of your "principal" investment of time and energy you expend to start and maintain your network of relationships. Additionally, those relationships could, but do not have to result in financial benefit.

A bond ladder is a strategy where you put together a group of financial investment bonds that have different maturities so that there will always be something providing income at different times. For example, if someone needed a monthly income of X amount of dollars, every month there would be a bond that comes due that would produce cash flow to meet that obligation.

Another great thing about high-quality bonds is that they can create a safety net in one's portfolio because they're viewed as less volatile than other asset classes such as stocks and real estate. If you can accumulate enough financial bonds to build a long-term ladder, you can have greater certainty of being able to cover your expenses over that time period. When a bond matures or comes due, the amount you invested returns to you, and you can then reinvest in another bond, effectively extending the length of the ladder. It is not uncommon for people to have ladders that continue for decades.

Although you don't get a cash payment for having a buddy, there are absolutely many benefits you receive from having social networks. Social networks allow us to thrive. They offer a mutual exchange of value, especially when you build a *diverse* network. This might look like successful people with whom you network with regularly; men and women ranging in age from their 20s to their 70s+. Through the years I have seen people who create *diverse* networks enjoy the rich assortment of insights and connections their circle of influence has helped them build. From better job opportunities to invitations to great sporting or entertainment events, a diverse network is a constant source of good surprises.

There is no question that staying in the workforce in some capacity offers advantages. Besides financial gain, you have the social structure that comes from your daily activities, your colleagues/friends, the feelings of accomplishment you get from doing things well and receiving praise—

the comradery. The trick is, if you are planning to retire, how can you replace this after you leave your job? Just like you need to replace your work income, you will also need to replace things that gave you regular encouragement, things so many of us enjoy, look forward to, and take advantage of during our work years. These all enhance your well-being daily. How do you recreate that solid social infrastructure once you exit from work?

I want to step back a little and examine why it's important to develop a buddy strategy. It seems that for a person over the age of 40, having a social network shouldn't be that difficult. But for most people, developing a social network outside of work can be daunting, especially when all of your identity evolves from what you do, where that happens, and in what capacity you do it.

What we're recognizing is that there is a definite value to having buddies at every stage of life. Older adults with diverse networks overall have a higher level of morale. Individuals with friends in their lives are reported to have greater longevity, and generally are healthier and less susceptible to things like stress, high blood pressure, dementia, anxiety and depression.[32] We want to keep that.

Historical Family Structure

When we look at social networks apart from our work environment, it's interesting to note how the dynamics have changed over past centuries. In the 1700s and early 1800s, families were together not only because they provided emotional support, love and other positive feelings for one another, but also out of necessity. Think back to what you may have learned in school about the period before the Industrial Revolution. People were largely generating a way of living through agriculture. It was necessary to not only have a family, but ideally to have large families with several members who could contribute to work, helping generate income from farming and harvesting crops.

Families were necessary for survival. It would be very hard for a household of four to create an economy of scale and the economic value needed to survive in the mid-1800s. Families stuck together and had the mission of growing for survival reasons as well as for emotional love and support.

People grew their own food, then harvested, cooked and served it up on the table—literally from farm to fork! Enter the Industrial Age. People started getting industrial related jobs that often paid enough that you could go somewhere else and get your food, such as the local market. Someone else planted and harvested for you. If you were near a diner, they also cooked for you. All you needed was income to pay for their services.

Although work lifestyles changed, many families continued to live near each other. Some even continued to pool resources and help each other financially when needed. However, they primarily stayed together to maintain their sense of kinship. The purpose of family relationships now became more centered on love and support.[33]

Skip ahead to the 1960s when the divorce rate began to rise significantly. Family members started to break apart, and became less reliant on each other for emotional support and financial stability. During this period people became more independent individuals.

You started seeing households dwindle down to two generations—parents and their children—and maybe a grandparent lived there after the children left. Although multiple-generations families are increasing (33%), we seldom see multiple generations of families living under the same roof as they did prior to the Industrial Age. As we advance more in society, we also see that families are smaller because large families are no longer needed for survival. People are also more conscious about global overpopulation, and various methods of birth control are readily available that can limit family size.

We get to the present and observe a very interesting dynamic emerging. Families are smaller and, as coincidentally, when we *exit from work*, we find ourselves with fewer kinships than ever before. Even the ones we have may not be close, either geographically, emotionally connected or both. There are no modern circumstances that force us to spend time with relatives we don't like or with whom we don't have much in common.

Fact: The 21st-century retiree exits work with fewer social and economic safety nets from family. For many, there is no longer an established group of supporters to provide memories, laughter and joy. In addition, there may be no one with whom to share resources to lower costs or help financially if an emergency occurs.

Your Best Network Is the One You Create

You may think, "Okay, Gregg, so where does laddering buddies come into all of this?" Well, once upon a time, just as people received support from strong nuclear families necessary for them to thrive, in the 21st century, as we exit from work, we are tasked with creating our own social relationships. I would argue that if you only develop social relationships within your cohorts, that is, people among your own age group, as you get older you could be the only one left standing. No one knows their own mortality, nor the mortality of individuals in their social network. If everyone you know is your age, you may be without the emotional support needed for greater wellness, health and well-being if everyone passes before you do. By sprinkling your network with a diversity of age ranges, you can greatly diminish the likelihood that you'll be the sole survivor of your social family.

When I mention laddering buddies, one thing that is very important as we look at the 21st-century exit is making sure that we have friendships that replace kinships, and that those friendships are multi-generational. It is important that we are supporting someone—a colleague or two—ahead of us in age, as well receiving and giving support from one or two generations behind us.

There are great benefits to having multigenerational friendships and networks. These social connections are good for us for two reasons. For one, we have someone that is interested in us, making us feel fulfilled, like we have a purpose, and as though we still matter. But the second and perhaps greater reason is that they create a sense of joy and accomplishment, a sense of psychological success that we get from helping each other out, similar to that which we got from work.

When we talk about helping others, this is about going from money to mission, where you're doing volunteer work, giving back to the community with your social time and capital. It can come in the form of just being close to your family members, helping your children raise their children, or tending to your parents who may be ailing. If your family isn't nearby, you can help out and in a way "adopt" a proxy family in the community.

When my son was younger, he played football after school. Practice for his team started at 3:30 pm, and the park the team played in was not within walking distance for him and several of his teammates. Also, his practice took place when most parents were working. This presented a challenge for many families who did not have family members to drive the kids or couldn't afford to hire a transportation service to drive their children.

There were a few kids on the team who I thought were being transported by their grandparents. My wife and I often discussed how lucky those kids' parents were to have such regular loyal support. On game days, when their entire families were present, I learned that many of the older people were not grandparents, but neighbors or former colleagues. They had engaged in Thriver behavior and extended their networks to include younger couples. This resulted in a win-win as they received love as if they were grandparents, and parents and football players received an immeasurable amount of love and support at a critical time.

Sometime later I saw a retired colleague in the grocery store. She told me the furniture store where she'd been working part-time had closed and she needed more to do during the day. She was caring for a preschool child in the morning and happily volunteered to drive my son to school when necessary. I never understood how she made money, because she only wanted reimbursement for gas. When I factored in what she spent cooking breakfast for both children, even though my son had already eaten, and buying Christmas toys, I know her financial return was negative. However, her social, emotional return was very positive–my family gave her joy and purpose. She could also benefit by interacting with his generation and mine. Our Boomer,

Generation X, and Generation Z collaboration created a win-win-win for us all.

The importance of developing a multi-generational environment or even "ecosystem" as I like to call it, is good for ourselves and even necessary for us to get the most out of our *exit from work*. Just like those financial bond ladders, we're laddering relationships. There always has to be those significant human connections in our circles who regularly exchange support of all kinds—both professionally and personally. Just as our bond ladder allows us to predict with some certainty what our income will be from the return on our investment, we also need to put together a mix of diverse individuals who can become near and dear to us. They don't have to be family members, but definitely should be people whom we enjoy being around. These significant people provide us with mutual exchanges of value, where we feel good when we're with them and hopefully, they feel good when they're with us.

Looking at my personal situation, my wife and I have couples with whom we go on double dates that range from 20 years younger than us to 20 years older. We enjoy all these relationships. Not only do we *ladder* our social relationships with these buddies, but we also think about creating future relationship ladders of support that we may need later on.

There currently are certain things that you may well be able to do for yourself - things you enjoy doing because you're mobile and healthy enough to do them. For example, you may mow the grass now, but will you feel like doing that ten years from now? How about 20 years from now? It would be helpful to develop relationships with others much younger than you, because when you turn 70 or 80, the people apt to be in your peer group will most likely not feel like mowing the grass, either.

Therefore, it's truly important to have those younger individuals in your life, not necessarily to just mow your grass, but to help in ways they wish to help. Here, I refer to the proverb, "Don't look a gift horse in the mouth." A gift is just that–a gift that's especially appreciated because it was unexpected. Your friends, chosen wisely, become your resource network to staying current with culture, understanding how things work and helping you stay engaged with the world at large—all valuable commodities of that relationship.

Note: Older cohorts are also very important from a wisdom standpoint.

Here, you continue to have a rich exchange of value. But you have to plan for this vibrant network. Start by creating a vision around it. For some, that may be a little challenging. Especially if you come from a work environment that was hierarchical. Boomers, especially, may have come from environments where seniority was most highly valued. Until recent times, senior leaders had meetings with one another and made all of the major business decisions. Their interactions were pretty much limited among other senior leaders. Everyone else stayed in their areas or departments, interacting within their cohort/colleague circles.

That model no longer works. Now it's essential to create multigenerational exchanges. You may ask, "How do I develop this multi-generational network if I'm not used to it? What if I'm only used to talking to my buddies from college or just to my siblings and cousins?" Or perhaps you feel, "I'm only used to working in my company, my industry and my community where they're just people like me. How do I break through the cycle and figure out how to develop this new model of relationships?"

First, step outside of your comfort zone. This starts with developing a vision. The nice thing about the Third Age is that it's an opportunity for you to figure out what you want to be on your terms. Once you've figured that out, you're not limited. This is about you seeing yourself rather than being at the end of something, but at the beginning of something unique and rewarding. You're boundaryless in what you can accomplish—if you're willing to go for it. It's no longer one of those things like when you were in elementary school where, if you enjoyed being around older kids, your teacher told you to stay away from them because, "They're more mature than you!"

Now, nothing is holding you back. It's up to you. Envision what you would like to be and do, and even how long you would like to do it. Then figure out who you would need to help you as you continue on your new path.

For instance, if you enjoy golfing every day, you need at least one person to play with, otherwise it could be very boring. As you *exit from work* and your free time grows, so does that of others in your cohort. They may decide to spend part of the year somewhere else, and suddenly you find yourself looking for someone to replace them.

Maybe you've been looking for a new golf buddy with no success. But now that you know the power of a diverse network, it's time to look beyond your neighborhood. For instance, you might create the perfect foursome with the millennial you're mentoring at work, the Gen Xer who was just added to your work team, a new Boomer from your church and you. This new group just may end up being your best golf buddies ever!

As you look at places in your community either through your park district, place of worship or other groups, after you form your vision, get very intentional about how you develop relationships with people in your environment. It might be a bit intimidating at first to get to know people in other age ranges, but they're just people, no matter how old they are. You can probably find a common interest or two. It's important to step outside of your comfort zone and make these connections because you will need this multi-generational group to help you move forward.

Reach out to your community. Start something that could go beyond your network and even help others create their circles of support so they have that buoyancy, too. One of my good friends formed a fantastic golf league that has withstood the test of time.

Building a great network is beneficial at any age, but I argue that it is even more important as you grow older. Studies have shown that people with adequate social relationships have a 50% lower mortality risk compared to those who report poor social relationships. A 2006 study found that giving emotional support to others was directly linked to lower blood pressure. Also, participants who reported giving support were also more likely to receive reciprocal support, and had greater feelings of self-esteem, self-efficacy and lower levels of depression.

Be intentional as you exit. Create a network where you're supported and you can give support to others. It may take some work. Consider starting your own Meetup Group. It won't feel natural or organic at first, because what naturally used to happen is you had your family somewhere near you, perhaps right next door, especially if you lived in a small town. Your family was everything. Now your family has either scattered far and wide and/or is smaller and you've got to create this for yourself.

Spouses and older children are now a central source of support for older people. For those born in 1900, by the time they turned 30, only 21% had any living grandparents.

For those born 100 years later in 2000, when they turn 30, 76% of them will have a living grandparent. The point is, even though your family may be smaller, because people are living longer, there are more people your grandparents' age out there. Therefore, the opportunity for multi-generational reach exists - you've just got to work at it. I don't know that most people recognize the importance of working at it, but it is critical. Who doesn't have a friend that supports someone they're not related to as they're aging, or is being supported by someone they're not related to as they're aging? Even if it's just a small task where that person comes by once a week and goes to the grocery store or performs other errands for them.

Finally, get rid of the mental barrier that someone is too young or too old to be a near and dear friend. Don't procrastinate - take a few minutes today and start getting comfortable talking with someone younger or significantly older than you that can become a friend and ally. This can be a colleague or someone in your neighborhood. Think of those hobbies you used to have before you put work ahead of all else. It's time to connect to those with similar interests and values to yours. Get beyond those mental walls that stop you from meeting new people who, within a short amount of time, can become more than just acquaintances. They will be your friends, perhaps even your new *extended family*. In all sincerity, your life may truly depend on this.

Three Action Takeaways

1) If you don't currently have a "Buddy Ladder" of folks on either side of the age spectrum from yourself, look around and find some with whom you can begin developing friendships now. Building trust and friendship takes time, so it's impossible to do this too early. It's an activity that is worthwhile, and can provide all concerned with mutual support and rewards. So get growing your Buddy Ladder, and have fun as you do.

2) If you greatly enjoy a certain age group of young people, identify that demographic, and what it is about engaging with them that makes you happy. Maybe your grandkids (if you have them) are already adults, or don't live in close proximity to you. Should that be the case, look around in your community for opportunities to volunteer for activities that you know you'll enjoy.

This could be coaching Little League or Peewee Football, teaching art, maybe volunteering to go on school field trips when the teacher in charge might need an additional adult because all of the parents are working and can't take off during the day. Check with your local Boys and Girls Club, possibly set up an appointment to talk with the elementary, middle school or high schools in the area about any needs for volunteerism that you could fill. It's a good idea to scope these opportunities out before you retire, if possible, so you can get on their radar as a volunteer down the road. But you might find that some of these (like kids' clubs, etc.) could put you in service right now, on the weekends. In whatever capacity they need someone like yourself, get involved when it's appropriate for you. This can be a great source of personal reward, so check it out.

3) Are you considering going back to school to pick up some new skills that you're confident will fit with your exit from work? If so, great! Check into whether you can audit a class (or at least one session of a class) to get a more fleshed out feel/appreciation for what the class or certification can bring you, and what skills you already have that will enhance your journey. If you know other retirees who have gone back to school in a field that differed from their career path, interview them over a cup of coffee or lunch; ask about how they got started, what motivated them, and what they love most about their results. They may become a mentor for you; at the very least, they will inspire you and give you their real-world experience for your consideration about your own pursuits.

CHAPTER 7: DISCOVERING YOUR FINANCIAL STRENGTH

Whether you're retired or working, money still makes the world go around. That's why it's difficult to discuss exiting from work without considering money—especially when you think about the changing financial issues surrounding retirement. In Chapter 1, we discussed several myths around retirement and the fact that several safety nets once in place no longer exist. It also points out certain views of others about commitments to our retirement success that may not be correct.

Even if they were, our lifestyles and life spans have changed; therefore, we need to make our resources, both social and economic, last longer. There is a greater amount of personal responsibility we must take for our future, and possibly in caring for older loved ones. This could leave you asking, "Haven't I been a grown up long enough? When do I get a few perks?"

Many of us feel something coming but don't know what to expect. There may be feelings of pressure as we receive reminders, whether or not intentional, that the time for work transition grows closer day by day, month by month, year by year. Frequently throughout my career I have watched younger colleagues enthusiastically say to older workers, "Aren't you glad you don't have to be here much longer? I bet you can't wait to retire." They usually intend this statement to be flattering.

The younger workers are often envious because they wish they could have more freedom instead of having to serve another 20 to 30 years in the prison they know as work, and on the boss's terms. Although they enjoy having a career, the idea of more time with family, longer vacations and the freedom to pursue more personal interests is appealing.

In their attempt to congratulate their coworker for getter closer to the freedom to exit work, they unfortunately may issue one of the greatest insults of that person's career. Unintentionally, they may send their older friends and coworkers a negative message. What was meant as a complement could easily be interpreted as:

- You're getting old
- You can't handle the rigor of a changing work environment
- Wouldn't someone your age prefer to do something safe and simple?
- It's time for you to leave
- Your value is diminishing

- You're not wanted here—take the retirement package and be happy.

For many, this brings up negative feelings because we know we have value. We know we still have much to contribute. We fear we are only being allowed to exist in a workplace instead of truly being included in its culture, ideals, innovation and success. Our thoughts may turn to, "When should I leave?" "Can I afford to leave?" or "Will they encourage me to leave or even push me out?"

Whether we are exiting by choice or being forced out, thinking about the money we'll need going into retirement isn't easy. Many people have complicated relationships with money. According to *Psychology Today*, money is the number one cause of divorce. And, 75% of Americans identify money as their number one source of stress.[34] An unhealthy relationship with money can reduce relationship satisfaction, worsen depression, and lead to emotional problems, health difficulties, and poor work performance.

Unfortunately, knowing this doesn't help much. Human beings often avoid facing their fears even when they know and acknowledge they could eliminate their fears if they did so!

Sue made good money as a journalist. She put away the full amount allowed in her 401k and she didn't even look at the amount she had in savings. She was frugal to the point that her friends wondered if she needed to take on another job.

In Sue's mind she was "poor" even though she had more than most. She didn't like looking at her bank balance, and rarely balanced her checkbook. Out of sight, out of mind, she thought.

Sue had grown up with parents who didn't talk about money, nor did they teach her about it. She only felt shame around it. It wasn't until she became engaged in her early 40s that she was forced to think about and look at money. Her fiancée Bill, a CPA, insisted on discussing money, retirement, and debt once they got engaged. Sue bit her lip and handed him her statements. She burst out crying and confessed she had no idea what kind of shape her money was in. She owned her car, and paid all her bills on time, she said. But she had no idea about anything else. With some trepidation Bill opened the statements and took a look at her net worth. He was pleasantly surprised. Between them they could both retire very comfortably at age 50.

Over the next three years Bill worked with Sue and a therapist to get at the root of Sue's fears about money. He taught her how to budget, how to track her investments, and how to set goals for herself and what she wanted her money to do for her. Her therapist worked through family issues and how she'd been raised to feel and think about money. It took time, and Sue says she's still working on her fears, but that things are so much better than they were. She and Bill pay bills together, "In case anything ever happens to him and I have to do it myself," she said. "I hate thinking that might happen, but it's better I learn now than if something did happen."

Unfortunately, most of us won't encounter someone like Bill, who will lead us through our financial fears. But we can take classes, consult an advisor, see a therapist, read a book and start nibbling away at those money fears at a pace we can stand. We need to do just that if we're ever going to realize a healthy exit from work.

As a result of our fears, many people do not think about the financial implications of exiting work until retirement is fast approaching and it's "too late" to save what they'll really need to make a healthy exit. As a financial advisor, I often counsel people about retirement. As part of an exercise I give them, they collect financial documents they seldom look at such as bank statements, investment statements, insurance policies and healthcare benefits booklets. They bring those to me to analyze. When we meet to discuss the results, I often start by telling them if they are in a good place financially so they can relax during the rest of the meeting. Most times I've learned that, like Sue, they are unaware of their financial position before I tell them.

Many people know they have been using a few good techniques, such as paying their mortgage on time, or contributing to their employer sponsored retirement plan.

However, they have been afraid to look at everything together and ask themselves "Do I have enough?" The reason they're afraid is if the answer is "no," the next question is "What am I going to do?" That second question can be downright frightening, especially if you feel you have little time to figure out an answer.

I once met a gentleman named Roy who was in his late 50s. Roy was stressing out about having enough money to support himself after he quit working. He had recently learned that his company's pension plan was going away, so he needed to start being more responsible for his financial future. Roy was a "Follower" in that he didn't plan financially or emotionally for his next stage in life. He went to work regularly and like Sue, rarely envisioned life beyond the work week.

When he started at his company, he signed up for several benefits he could not recall. He took part in a 401k plan, which automatically invested money from his paychecks, but could not remember what he invested in or why. Roy felt it was customary to work until his mid-60s, and then basically let the chips fall where they may—allow whatever was meant to happen, happen to him. He did not take ownership of his future. Instead he believed that the system or others would provide a perfect roadmap for him to follow, like other retirees before him.

The elimination of the company's pension plan was a wake-up call for Roy. He came to see me based on a recommendation from a friend. I asked him to collect various documents that would help us analyze his investments, cash flow, health insurance and other items. Obviously terrified throughout the entire process, Roy kept saying, "I hope I'll be okay." Our analysis showed that Roy had a high probability of financial success if he retired based upon the age he planned to do so, the lifestyle he wanted to live, and the projected resources that would be available.

What was interesting to me was that he had benefits he was unaware of, such as a health savings account and company stock. After he got a good understanding of his financial position, he was greatly relieved. When I asked him why he had never looked at his total financial picture, he said it was too overwhelming. He trusted his employer to provide for him as it had done so for those who retired before him. Roy told me his friend insisted he come see me. I asked him, "Why didn't you seek financial help on your own before this?" He replied, "I was afraid that I might hear bad news."

Roy and Sue were very fortunate to have enough resources to support their futures. However, what if they didn't? Without the influence of his friend, the gap between Roy's assets and ideal financial position could have grown further apart each year. Although Roy was very intelligent and successful, he avoided becoming financially literate.

This seems odd for a skilled and educated person, but it happens more often than you might think. According to researchers at George Washington University, approximately 70% of the U.S. adult population is financially illiterate.[35] This includes people who have money–in some cases a lot of money!

Our lack of financial literacy comes from not having financial courses as a formal part of most school curriculums, or not having a role model to teach us informally about money. Given the reduced number of financial safety nets, such as Roy's employer's pension plan, it is important for us to advance from Followers to Thrivers regarding our retirement financial future. Remember, Thrivers take responsibility and control of their situations. They take the time to learn new things or find people who can assist them. The good news is it's never too late to learn. If you feel it is too late, you may be wrong because you may get a life bonus and more time to figure things out. Here are a few basic things you can do to build your financial strength as you prepare for your next act:

Pay yourself first. The most common ways people build wealth are through their home and employer sponsored retirement plans. The reason these are successful is that they are structured and require regular monthly discipline. If you contribute to a 401k or 403b plan, your employer takes that cash out and applies it to your monthly savings before they give you your paycheck. That way, you never risk being tempted to spend the money on other items.

Also, when prioritizing what bills to pay, most people pay their mortgage first, to ensure they have housing for their family. When you pay down your mortgage you are building equity in an asset you may be able to sell and convert to cash in the future. Banks often offer incentives such as lower interest rates for mortgage customers who pay them with an automatic debit from their checking account. Over time, most people build a discipline and don't miss spending what they are contributing. The trick is to contribute as much as possible. A good guideline is to save 10% or more of your pre-tax income. If this is difficult, start with a lower amount and work your way up as your income increases. Also, use retirement accounts such as 401k, 403b, IRA or Roth IRA that provide tax savings. If you don't know what type of account to use, consult a qualified financial advisor to provide guidance.

Take advantage of matching funds from your employer. Many employers match what you save in your employer sponsored plan up to a certain amount. For example, your employer may match every $1 you save up to 6% of your pay. If you make $50,000, your employer will contribute $1 to match every dollar you put in your account up to $3,000 ($50,000 x 6% = $3,000). You get a 100% return on the first $3,000 your put in the account. Where else can you get a 100% guaranteed return? You can't – so why miss the opportunity. Pay yourself and get all you can with your employer's matching funds. Also, money invested in certain qualified employer sponsored retirement plans goes into your account income tax free and grows tax free until you withdraw it.

Understand your expenses. Many people don't know where their money goes every month. Have you ever been shocked when you open your credit card bill and it was higher than you anticipated? A cup of coffee cost $3, however we often forget how many times we go to the coffee shop in a month. I recently watched a good commercial where someone was asked how many subscription services like movie streaming, music and newspapers they get charged for each month, and how often they use the services. The person in the commercial quickly realizes he forgot how many services he has. He also realizes he is paying for services he no longer uses.

Understand what you're investing in. Things worked out for Roy and Sue, mentioned earlier. Lucky for them both the investments they picked when they signed up for their respective retirement plans performed well over time. However, I have also seen things go the other way for people. When I worked for a commercial bank, I once received a phone call from someone who was driving his daughter to college. It was her first year of school and they were very excited. He told me he needed funds wired to the school for her tuition. He said he had deposited funds in a money market account when she was a little girl, and it should have grown to the amount needed. When I told him his account balance, he began to panic because he did not have enough.

Interest rates had fallen significantly from the time he opened the account; therefore he did not earn as much as he projected. The account he had was taxable, which also lowered his returns. He did not understand the type of account he had invested in, or if there may have been a better option for college savings. It's okay if you don't know finance—you're far from alone. However, get proactive and engage in Thriver behavior now. Seek qualified investment advice. Also, meet with your advisor at least annually to make sure you're on track to reach your goal, or if you need to make adjustments.

Make a budget and stick to it. Many people dislike budgets because they require you to be accountable to yourself and/or your partner. A budget examines your cash inflows (salary, bonuses, etc.) and your cash outflows (mortgage, rent, car payment, entertainment, etc.). The goal is for your inflows to be greater than your outflows so you will have more room to save money for your future. Here's a little secret–most wealthy people have a budget! Warren Buffett, Bill Gates, Oprah Winfrey, and so on all hire accountants and financial professionals to help them manage and keep track of their cash inflows and outflows. They started with small budgets and now they have large ones.

When building wealth, it's not how much money you make, it's how much money you keep!

Work with your partner. There is a saying that goes "It takes teamwork to make a dream work." If you have a spouse or partner you need to work as a team to reach your retirement dream. A recent study by Harris Poll showed that many couples are disconnected when saving for retirement.[36] In the study, 33% of Americans reported that they nor their partner is saving for retirement. Of those that save, only 43% consult with their partner before making trading decisions in their retirement accounts. Approximately 20% of individuals have not told their partner how much they save for retirement. In addition, less than 50% of couples have tried to calculate what they may need in retirement.

Separating financial responsibilities may work when you both are working. However, you may have to pool resources and rely on your partner for income or benefits in retirement. Assuming they will have a guaranteed pension or retiree health benefit may cause your household to experience a shortfall if you do not communicate with each other. Communication about finances can be more challenging as family structures become more complex. Couples with blended families may find it difficult to discuss financial obligations, especially if they are providing for individuals from a prior relationship. Avoiding tough conversations may seem easy now, however long-term this strategy may not be in your best interest.

These are a few basic tips; however, you may need many more based upon your circumstances. There is not a "one size fits all" solution for everyone trying to build their financial strength. It is important to work with trusted advisors such as your accountant, financial advisor and attorney to identify the best practices and solutions for you.

A Thriver is the architect of their own future and seeks to find the resources needed to make their best life happen. Don't avoid thinking about your future any longer. Take the time to ask friends and family members who they enjoy working with and why? Interview each professional to see if they are right for you. Also, check their credentials with the governing body that licenses them, such as the Certified Financial Planner Board of Standards, Securities and Exchange Commission and the Bar Association, to make sure there are no violations against them.

Do I Have Enough?

In the earlier example, Roy waited until the end of his career before learning to understand his financial position. Ultimately, it turned out that he was in a good position to *exit from work* on his own terms. If you can understand how to create a good financial strategy and have enough time to execute it, that will lead to a higher probability of success in retirement. Unfortunately, everyone will not be as lucky as Roy. Many people approaching work exit realize late in the game that they don't have the financial strength they desire, and little time to bridge their financial gaps. If you fall into that category, the good news is there is still hope. It just means you will have to work harder to make things work.

Becoming financially literate is important no matter what your stage of life. In a 2011 study, 88% of near retirees rated receiving financial advice as they approached retirement as important.[37] If you don't have as much time as you would like to grow your financial nest egg, late stage financial literacy can help you correct parts of your course to achieve better outcomes. It can also provide you with tools to educate your children so they don't make the same mistakes. You should feel better knowing you and your family are now on a path to achieve wealth for future generations if you desire.

Becoming more educated about financial issues is the first step towards developing your financial strength, but financial empowerment requires more. Gaining a financial understanding is good, absolutely. However, many people are uncomfortable making career transitions because of their fear of uncertainty. Even households with great income, budgetary discipline and capacity to save can have anxiety related to money. Although they are building their prosperity, they cannot control investment returns, inflation rates, tax rates, and policy changes that may impact their wealth.

One of my colleagues shared a story with me about a client who has meaningful wealth but is afraid to transition into part-time or full-time retirement although he would very much like to. The advisor went through multiple retirement scenarios with him, such as what if a severe recession or critical illness occurs. The analysis showed he has a high probability of financial success in each case. Although the data makes a credible argument, he still worries about running out of money.

Based on his spending level, it is unlikely that he will run out of money in retirement. However, because he constantly worries about uncertainty and things he cannot control, will he fully thrive in retirement? There are a few financial guidelines that he can follow that have worked for retirees in the past. I'll share some with you here:

Limit your annual spending to 3 to 5% of your savings. This guideline may vary based on your annual spending needs and how your assets are invested. Consult with your financial advisor before using it to make sure it is appropriate for you.

Maintain a healthy lifestyle. Healthcare is one of the largest expenses in retirement. Households average $122,000 in medical expenses between age 70 and death.[38]

Maintaining a healthy lifestyle lowers the chance of your retirement nest egg being reduced by unanticipated medical expenses.

Insure against catastrophic events that can reduce your savings. Medicare does not cover all medical expenses. Additional insurance through Medicare supplement policies and long-term care policies can help provide costs if skilled nursing and/or assisted living is needed in the future. Also, adequate levels of property insurance are necessary to replace assets you cannot afford to pay for when you stop working.

Although these guidelines have worked in the past, no one can say with 100% certainty they will work in the future, because the future is unknown. Although the client in the above example appears to be financially ready, he still struggles because he cannot let go of the worries that prevent him from being a Thriver. Thrivers live their best life because they access a newfound freedom that comes with later life wisdom, resources, changed responsibilities and a longer lifespan. So, what is the client lacking, and how can he achieve it to gain greater life satisfaction and freedom?

Financial Self-Efficacy

Self-efficacy is a term more commonly used in academic environments. Dr. Albert Bandura is a psychologist and researcher. He is credited for developing our understanding of self-efficacy and how it factors in certain decisions. Self-efficacy refers to a sense of personal agency. It represents a person's belief that they can achieve and succeed at a given task.[39] It relates to self-confidence, motivation, optimism and the belief that a person can cope with a variety of life changes. People with high levels of self-efficacy believe they can perform well at a specific task. This may not be true for every task. For example, a person may have a high level of self-efficacy in their profession but may struggle to manage their personal budget or lose weight.

A person with high self-efficacy may have greater success over time because they believe in their ability to influence their destiny. In his book, *When Likes Aren't Enough: A Crash Course in the Science of Happiness,* professor and researcher Dr. Tim Bono gives an example of how two groups of individuals treated depression in a research study. In the study, individuals in one group treated their depression by taking antidepressant medication. Individuals in the second group treated their depression by increasing how much they exercised.

Over time, both groups had improvements in health and a lower incidence of depression. However, the group that treated their depression with exercise experienced results over a longer time period. This is not an argument to avoid proper counseling or not take medication when dealing with depression. The point is, people in the second group had better results because they believed they had greater control of the outcome than their peers who used medication. They were in control of their exercise program and schedule. They believed the outcome they wanted was driven by their behavior.

Financial Self-Efficacy encompasses a person's ability or belief that they can complete certain financial tasks or be successful in certain financial situations. A person can have great financial knowledge, but if they do not have the discipline, ability or belief in themselves to do things such as budget or control spending they will lack financial self-efficacy. Improving your financial self-efficacy requires an understanding that you are not powerless in financial situations just because you have exited work.

Although you left your job behind, you did not leave your skills, network and other resources that make you awesome! If anyone suggests you are old—you know better. You can do more if you choose and should always think about how you can go into action if needed. You can return to your career, start a business, or go back to school and start a new career. Individuals with high levels of self-efficacy believe that they can accomplish difficult tasks and cope with adversity. Self-efficacy motivates people to set goals and take action when they perceive there may be barriers or setbacks.[40]

Increasing Self-Efficacy

You may wonder, "If self-efficacy is a benefit, how do I get more of it?" Bandura names four sources of efficacy beliefs.[41]

Mastery of experiences. Being successful in financial situations will build confidence and financial self-efficacy. How can you accomplish this if you feel you have limited financial knowledge or ability? You can start with small victories and work your way up. For example, if you are not good with your annual budget, start by setting daily budgets. I often coach clients by having them put their receipts from daily purchases in their pocket and reviewing them every evening while asking themselves, "Was this purchase necessary?" Building mastery with daily expenses expands to mastery of weekly and eventually annual expenses.

If you haven't saved a large enough nest egg, do you believe you have the skills to work longer? Of course you do! However, work with your financial advisor to identify the timeframe and savings strategy so you feel more in control. Working in retirement has become a solution for individuals who need to delay spending down their savings to make their retirement assets last longer.

The addition of a few years of some form of enjoyable part-time or full-time work can reduce the need for withdrawals from savings targeted for full retirement and allow retirement assets to have additional compound growth.

This is especially beneficial if retirement assets are in an account that provides tax advantages, such as a 401k, 403b or IRA.

Applying the "Rule of 72" shows why the addition of 10 to 15 years of enjoyable work to cover living expenses while your retirement nest egg grows may be worthwhile. (The Rule divides the number 72 by the annual rate of return to estimate how long it may take to double an investment).

Rate Of Return	Years To Double
5%	14.4
6%	12.0
7%	10.3
8%	9.0

Continuing to work may also provide some key employer-sponsored benefits, such as health and life insurance, which, if paid by you, could become more expensive in later years.[42]

Vicarious experiences. Observing our role models can increase our belief that we can be successful, too. When picking financial role models, we should be careful not to pick people based upon the fact that they have more assets than us, because we do not know the source of their assets. You may think someone is financially successful; however, they may have received a nice inheritance or a lucrative financial settlement.

Hanging out with them may only make you more socially competitive and tempt you to spend more while struggling to "keep up with the Joneses." Instead, should pick financial role models who you think make good decisions. Ask yourself if they are impulsive spenders, or do they wait for great deals and discounts? How do they reinvent themselves when they change jobs or careers? When they want something, do they just go for it, or do they make calculated decisions? What makes them successful?

Verbal persuasion. Surround yourself with people you respect who can build you up on your journey. Build social bonds with buddies that encourage you to win. This can come from parents, siblings, friends, coworkers or someone you pick as a coach. Being persuaded that we can accomplish certain things often results in us putting forth more effort to master them. How many of us know people who are successful because they moved away from people who told them what they couldn't accomplish in favor of associations with people who told them what they *could* accomplish?

Emotional state. The state you are in will affect your self-efficacy in general as well as when building your financial strength. Maintaining a positive and healthy state of mind is important. Depression and stress can contribute negatively to your self-belief, whereas positive emotions can move us closer to our goals.

Imaginal experiences. Psychologist James Maddux has suggested a fifth factor that is also important. To have the best chance of achieving something, visualize yourself taking the actions to get there and also having a successful outcome. If you have a spouse or partner, you should also work together on any shared visions that you both support.

Learn to set financial boundaries with friends and family. Once I see clients become more financially solvent and in control I sometimes notice friends and family without the same discipline begin to want to borrow or access the savings their family member or friend has. If you have, or had a hard time managing money before, the pressure to "help" others may derail you. Learn to say no to requests for help, or to evaluate those requests and see them as healthy or unhealthy investments and purchases just like any other. Many people who grow up watching poor or non-existent money and financial boundaries often experience poor personal boundaries as well. When you see your wealth accumulating you may also feel a need to spend more, either because you feel guilty or entitled to treat yourself. Money is so much more than just numbers. It can be an emotional roller-coaster as well. If you struggle with feelings about your money, and your shift in how you manage it, don't be afraid to seek counseling or help to examine and resolve those feelings.

Three Action Takeaways

1) Face your financial fears. Sue and Roy both were afraid to look at their net worth and financial statements because they feared they might not have enough money. The ocean doesn't stop coming in just because you bury your head in the sand. Whether you need to sit down with a financial advisor, a therapist, family member with good financial boundaries and skills, or your spouse, face your fears.

2) Educate yourself. It can be scary to think about, look at, or understand your accounts, your income, savings, or investments. Educate yourself through classes, books, or talking to a good financial advisor. The more you understand the more likely you are to be able to eliminate your fears around money.

3) Make money a game. If you're intimidated by money, investments, and all the big words you hear or read about money, start simple. Buy or sign up for money classes offered for children. The terms and descriptions are geared towards children and are often less threatening and intimidating for adults with little or no financial awareness. You can move at your own pace and build your confidence as you go. Playing games with themes around money can

make learning and practicing things like budgets and investments more fun.

CHAPTER 8: EXIT OPTIONS

It's always nice to have options. The pattern of prior generations made it seem like there was only one path when exiting from work. You worked 30+ years and then retired to a life of leisure and rest. For some people, this is still a preferred choice. However, for others it won't be ideal. Age 60 is now middle age and much too early to limit yourself to a rocking chair, bingo, and travel.

I once asked a gentleman in his 70s why he hadn't retired after working 50 years at the same company. He said he believed, "You should retire *to* something, not *from* something." Makes perfect sense. He was afraid of having a life without structure, purpose and meaning, so he postponed leaving his employer until he could find another environment that could replace it. The one thing he was certain of was sitting at home collecting his pension and social security checks was not the answer. Although he could afford several activities to keep him busy during the day such as golf, travel and dining out, that wasn't enough. If you are struggling to find what to retire to, here are few non-traditional things you may want to consider.

Going Back to College

As you think about returning to school, memories of your glory days on campus may wash over you, or conversely might strike a bit of terror in you, remembering that test you failed. I'm not trying to take you back in time, but instead, make you aware that college has become much more fun in ways that benefit older people since you left. I'm not suggesting a lifestyle of sophomoric adventures like Rodney Dangerfield's character pursued in the 1987 movie *Back to School*, or creating your own fraternity like in the 2003 movie *Old School*. However, the nice thing about being able to structure your next act in life in the 21st century is that anything is possible.

In recent years, several colleges and universities have created university-based retirement communities (UBRCs). The term UBRC was coined in 2006 by Andrew Carle at George Mason University.[43] University based retirement communities are relatively new, and the level of services and engagement between the living community and the college or university may vary depending on the school.

The communities provide living facilities near or on campus where residents can interact with other alumni or people who identify with the school. Each college or university is different, but on average, approximately 10% of residents are alumni. There may be a range of housing options from independent living to memory care. Communities are structured for individuals who want to remain socially and intellectually stimulated. Members of the community can audit classes, teach, volunteer or find employment at the university. There is also access to health clubs, golf courses and sporting events at the school to create work-life balance on your terms.

This model can create a win-win for everyone. University communities can be great places for individuals who are looking for a new but familiar community with options for work, social relationships, entertainment, intellectual growth, and generativity. In addition, the schools benefit by having stronger relationships with their alumni and a community who can support them. Today there are over 100 programs near or at different schools across the country such as Stanford, Cornell, the University of Florida, and the University of Arizona.[44] You can find a full list of schools with affiliations at https://www.retirementliving.com/college-linked-retirement-communities.

Internships or "Returnships"

The movie *The Intern* with Robert De Niro is a great comedy, but it's more than just a film–it represents the lifestyle of many older people trying to figure out their next act. De Niro's character in the 2015 movie is a 70-year-old widower who learns retirement is not all it's cracked up to be. As a result, he finds an internship to re-enter the workforce.

Internships are not just for young adults anymore; they are also for older individuals with life experiences that can help employers improve their businesses. "Returnships" are nine weeks to six-month internships for individuals who have been out of the workplace for two or more years and want to return.[45] The programs focus on professionals who have left the workforce for reasons such as parenthood, retirement, military service or to provide care for a loved one. Returnships are a good way to exit from a primary career, yet maintain aspects of your professional identity after taking a break.

The programs provide an opportunity for employers and employees to examine skill sets, values and other traits to see what is right for them. Returnships often lead to part-time or full-time job offers for participants. According to Path Forward, a nonprofit that focuses on helping people restart their careers, approximately 80% of its interns get hired into permanent roles.[46] Companies that have return-to-work programs include Goldman Sachs, J.P. Morgan, MetLife, General Motors and IBM. Returnships can be found through organizations such as iRelaunch and Path Forward.

Peace Corps

If you want to give back, see the world and don't mind working hard in different ways, the Peace Corps can be a rewarding way to exit from your primary career and find meaning and purpose. We typically think of the Peace Corps as a place for young volunteers; however, many people are not aware there is no age limit at many volunteer organizations. Approximately 6% of Peace Corps volunteers are age 50 or older.[47] In 2018 Kiplinger's reported an 83-year old woman as the organization's oldest volunteer.[48]

Assignments in the Peace Corps are typically more difficult than an average job, but they can provide life changing adventures and experiences not found in common places. In addition, the Peace Corps provides a few benefits that may be helpful as you gradually transition from work. Volunteers receive a modest housing stipend, and a transition fund around $8,000 when they complete their assignment. Although this will not grow your net worth, it may allow you to postpone using your retirement funds a few years while your assets grow. In addition, volunteers receive healthcare coverage, which can help bridge the gap to Medicare. Volunteers can also defer student loans if they have any at this stage. You can learn more about the wide variety of volunteer opportunities in the Peace Corps by visiting https://www.peacecorps.gov.

Entrepreneurship

Entrepreneurship is an attractive alternative for individuals seeking to exit from work gradually and on their own terms while maintaining as much or as little of their professional identity as they like. It also provides flexibility for individuals to select assignments, structure their workday, and negotiate their compensation.

One of my former colleagues loved photography as a hobby. After raising his family and practicing his career, he converted his hobby into his next stage career. He now casually travels with his backpack to different parts of the world and takes pictures for days at a time. When he returns, they display his wonderful work at art shows and galleries. I have even purchased a few pieces. He has successfully made his work his play and generated a few dollars in the process.

Although the success rate for new businesses has historically been low, which may be intimidating, the story is much different for older workers. According to researchers at Duke University, individuals over age 50 are twice as likely to be successful in technology start-up ventures than those under age 25.[49] Older individuals are often more successful as entrepreneurs because they have more financial strength, personal stability, and self-awareness than those in other age ranges. Things to consider before starting a business include:[50]

How much money will you need to invest to start a business? Although entrepreneurship may provide newfound freedom, it should not threaten the financial security you have worked long and hard to build. Before committing to a business, consult your financial advisor and discuss what types of business are appropriate for you.

What personal risk may come from your business? If you have had a full career as an employee, you may not have had to think about business liability and threats to your personal estate. By converting hobbies or other interests to a business requires protection beyond your homeowner's and personal umbrella policies. You should discuss your business plans with your attorney, insurance agent and other advisors and see whether the formation of an LLC, LLP, or corporation and the purchase of business insurance are advisable to protect the assets you have accumulated personally.

Will you have fun? Although you are starting a business, you are doing it as part of your retirement lifestyle. Retirement work is best when you get to do things you enjoyed at work, engage socially, achieve goals and build financial security. Make sure the venture you choose doesn't feel like work, but more like meaningful play.

Restructuring Work

Maybe you love what you currently do but want to do it differently. Renegotiating and restructuring your current role may be the change you want and need. It may also allow you to exit the workforce gradually if you can negotiate the terms you need. According to a survey by CareerBuilder, 30% of U.S. workers age 60 and older plan to work to age 70 or older.[51] The question is, "How do you negotiate terms that uniquely represent your needs and also provide an ongoing benefit to your employer?"

G. A. Finch is an attorney who focuses on negotiating executive employment agreements and providing strategic career advice. He is the author of the book *The Savvy Executive*. According to Mr. Finch, each situation is unique when negotiating terms for modifying your employment, and therefore, you should seek credible guidance before doing so. In general, here are a few things you should consider:

- Always view your relationship with your employer from the perspective of how it would benefit him or her. At the risk of stating the obvious, remember that your employment is an economic relationship, not a charitable one.

- Suggest to your employer that the newly configured role could be on a trial basis. This may minimize the risk to the employer and make your proposal of a modified role more palatable.

- Get imaginative about the mechanics and scope of the proposed arrangement, *e.g.*, be willing to do part-time work or telecommute. These have a more limited or expanded scope of work. You can be available on an as-needed consulting basis, or serve as a pinch hitter for emergencies.

- Offer additional, different or new services to the employer such as mentoring, blogging, doing business development, recruiting talent, doing neglected research, training employees, or leading a new business initiative.

- Suggest trading or adjusting your salary for performance-based equity or cash bonus awards, more time off, time for charitable service, time for a personal entrepreneurial endeavor, tuition reimbursement, private club dues, *etc.*–your suggestions are limited only by your imagination.

The surprising upshot here is that you may end up enjoying an extended tenure at your present employer.

Three Action Takeaways

1) Name three things you'd like to do if you decided to start a business. Do some research on what is actually involved in things like selling your crafts or vegetables online, or at your local farmer's market.

2) Imagine yourself going back to school. Get a catalog from your local community college and see what classes pique your interest. There may be a cooking

class, a wine making class, welding, or graphic art classes that catch your eye. Take a class just for fun to see how it feels.

3) Volunteer at your local zoo, or other business for a day, or a week to see what it's like. This could be working at a T-shirt shop or returning or interning at something that's always interested you.

CONGRATULATIONS ON BEING MORE EXIT-READY!

Exiting from work in the 21st century can be challenging because many terms and conditions of work and retirement have changed. As a result, a clear roadmap or model to follow may not exist. You may take a traditional approach to leisure or feel a little pressure as you trail blaze to what is right for you. Regardless, these can be the best days of your life because you now have the freedom from obligations to others such as raising a family, the wisdom and knowledge that comes with age, financial freedom from years of working, good health and the desire to thrive.

Approaching this time in your life with the most positive attitude possible may not make your transition into your next phase exactly seamless, but it will definitely help a lot. If you're still working and plan to retire anytime within the next three to five years, whatever you can do to pre-plan and lay some solid groundwork in advance of that "last day on the job" will help you feel better prepared, more positive, and should remove a good deal of stress. My hope is that the tips and case studies shared in this book have provided you with food for thought as well as some practical tools with which you can build a solid foundation for your retirement, however you choose to design and enjoy it.

The trick is to figure out who you are at this stage and what you want to be. I have presented a few options; just remember that your choices are endless and unlimited. The only boundaries you face are those created by lack of imagination and creativity. Getting some counseling or working with a life coach experienced in working with others at your stage are other choices that you may find helpful. Even if you've been in top tier management for several years, that doesn't mean that you completely have the best grip on how to successfully switch gears into retirement and feel good about the process. In fact, it's often harder for C-suite/top execs to release their familiar overload of responsibilities and to embrace their next act.

This will probably be your first retirement, and if you've never done it before, getting support and assistance is a wise path to take. There is no shame in seeking help when faced with new situations. Remember some of your early mentors when you were a fresh-faced "newbie" starting out on your first job. Someone hopefully took you under his/her wing and showed you the ropes. If they did, no doubt your life was enriched and made a bit easier by that. Standing at the precipice of a new adventure that just happens to be called "retirement" could be enhanced by getting a mentor experienced in that field, and/or finding wise counsel in a variety of ways. It's up to you and what you feel will work best with your particular talents and personality type.

Exit from work may mean no work at all for you, or what others may view as work, but you know as play. Make your next chapter in life the most rewarding of all as you find greater purpose, deeper meaning and make contributions to yourself, your family, your community and the world like never before. *What will the new you look like?*

ACKNOWLEDGEMENTS

I want to take a moment to recognize and offer a special thank you to Melissa G. Wilson, my publisher at Networlding Publishing. I greatly appreciated the many hours of her dedicated coaching and editing efforts. I also benefitted greatly from the support of Melissa's talented Networlding book-creation team who assisted me in writing, publishing, and now launching my book.

I'd also like to thank my friends and colleagues who served as beta readers of the book.

Finally, I offer a warm thanks to my photographer, Kimberly Mitchell of Candid Giggles (http://candidgiggles.com/).

BEFORE YOU GO

Thanks so much for allowing me to spend time with you as you read this book. I'd like to take just a few more minutes to make a small request.

If you enjoyed this book, gained even just a few insights that were helpful to you, please share them with others. I also invite you to share what you have learned with those inside and outside your family who you believe could benefit from this book.

But most of all, please share what worked for you on Amazon with a paragraph or two review. Amazon is where more than two thirds of all books are sold. I would sincerely welcome the insights you gleaned from reading *Exit From Work* to help you make better choices as to how to live your life to its fullest.

How to Leave a Review?

Just go to Amazon (www.amazon.com), look up the title *Exit from Work*, and type in a short review. Even if you only have read a couple of chapters, leaving reviews make all the difference to the success of a book. Your impressions and takeaways matter. Reviews truly make a difference for readers and the author.

In our content-cluttered world, books succeed by the kind, generous time readers take to leave honest reviews. I thank you in advance for this very kind gesture. And, finally, if you would like to reach out to me with questions or comments about the book, please feel free to email me at: AuthorGreggLunceford@gmail.com

NOTES

[1] Jing Jun Ma, "Your Odds of Dying by Age and Gender," Finder, updated November 7, 2019, finder.com/life-insurance/odds-of-dying.

[2] Lynda Gratton and Andrew Scott, *The 100-Year Life: Living and Working in an Age of Longevity* (London: Bloomsbury Publishing, 2017).

[3] Sally Kane, "Baby Boomers in the Workplace: How Their Generational Traits and Characteristics Affect the Workplace," The Balance Careers, updated October 7, 2019, https://www.thebalancecareers.com/baby-boomers-2164681.

[4] Gabriel H. Sahlgren, "Work Longer, Live Healthier: The Relationship between Economic Activity, Health and Government Policy," Institute of Economic Affairs, May 2013, iea.org.uk/wp-content/uploads/2016/07/Work%20Longer,%20Live_Healthier.pdf.

[5] Mike Lewis, "Life After Retirement: What Do I Do Now?" *Forbes,* October 22, 2013, forbes.com/sites/mikelewis/2013/10/22/life-after-retirement/#4e81e8d16777.

[6] "Benefits Planner: Retirement." Social Security Administration, accessed September 28, 2019, ssa.gov/planners/retire/r&m6.html.

[7] Todd Tressider, "12 Dangerous Retirement Myths That Turn Your Golden Years Into Lead," Financial Mentor,

accessed September 28, 2019, financialmentor.com/retirement-planning/retirement-myths/18185.

[8] Zack Friedman, "78% of Workers Live Paycheck to Paycheck," *Forbes,* January 11, 2019,

forbes.com/sites/zackfriedman/2019/01/11/live-paycheck-to-paycheck-government-shutdown/#3d0718a04f10.

[9] Greg Goth, "Early Retirement Health Care Quandary Keeps Workers on the Job," Society for Human Resource Management, July 31, 2017, shrm.org/resourcesandtools/hr-topics/benefits/pages/early-retiree-healthcare-quandary.aspx.

[10] Janice Lloyd, "Key to a Healthy, Happy Retirement: Having Fun," *USA Today,* October 21, 2013, usatoday.com/story/money/personal-finance/2013/01/29/boomer-health-retirement-second-act/1851271.

[11] Andrew T. Jebb, Louis Tay, Ed Diener, and Shigehiro Oishi, "Happiness, Income Satiation, and Turning Points around the World," *Nature Human Behavior* 2 (January 2018): 33–3, https://doi.org/10.1038/s41562-017-0277-0.

[12] Tim Bono, *When Likes Aren't Enough: Using the Science of Happiness to Find Meaning and Connection in a Modern World* (London: Seven Dials, 2018).

[13] Projects Abroad, "Volunteer Abroad for Over 50s," accessed September 29, 2019, projects-abroad.org/trip-format/grown-up-specials/?utm_campaign=vf-volunteer-abroad-opportunities-for-seniors-and-retirees&utm_medium=referral&utm_source=volunteerforever.com.

[14] Thomas Barrett, "Retirement Myths," Society for Psychotherapy, accessed September 29, 2019, societyforpsychotherapy.org/retirement-myths.

[15] Patrice Lee Onwuka, "They're Back! Share of Adult Children Living at Home Highest in 75 Years," Independent Women's Forum, April 12, 2018.

iwf.org/blog/2806275/They're-Back!-Share-of-Adult-Children-Living-at-Home-Highest-in-75-Years-

[16] Gini, A. (2004). Work, Identity and Self: How We Are Formed by The Work We Do. Journal of Business Ethics, 17(7), 707-714.

[17] Aly Weisman, "15 People Who Failed Before Becoming Famous," *Business Insider,* October 29, 2012, businessinsider.com/15-people-who-failed-before-becoming-famous-2012-10?op=1#jerry-seinfeld-was-booed-off-stage-4.

[18] Neuro Gym Team, "11 Wildly Successful Entrepreneurs Who Failed First," Neuro Gym, accessed September 29, 2019, blog.myneurogym.com/11-wildly-successful-entrepreneurs-who-failed-first.

[19] Bryan DeArdo, "NFL Stars Who Retired Early: Andrew Luck Joins List of 10 Other Great Players Who Stepped Away in Their Prime," *CBS Sports,* August 26, 2019, cbssports.com/nfl/news/nfl-stars-who-retired-early-andrew-luck-joins-list-of-10-other-great-players-who-stepped-away-in-their-prime/

[20] Jack Bechta, "NFL Is in Need of a Better Exit Plan for Its Players," National Football Post, accessed September 29, 2019, nationalfootballpost.com/nfl-is-in-need-of-a-better-exit-plan-for-its-players.

[21] History.com Editors, "Benjamin Franklin," updated October 22, 2019, https://www.history.com/topics/american-revolution/benjamin-franklin.

[22] Statista Research Department, "The Average Retirement Age in the United States from 1900 to 2010," Statista, June 4, 2014, statista.com/statistics/319983/average-retirement-age-in-the-us.

[23] RC Atchley, "Retirement as a Social Institution," *Annual Review of Sociology* 8 (1982), pp. 263–87, https://doi.org/10.1146/annurev.so.08.080182.001403.

[24] Jinhee Kim, Jasook Kwon, and Elaine A. Anderson, "Factors Related to Retirement Confidence: Retirement Preparation and Workforce Financial Education," *Association for Financial Counseling and Planning Education* 16, no. 2 (2005), 77–89, https://psycnet.apa.org/record/2006-11386-006.

[25] McFarland, B. (2016, February 18). A Continuing Shift in Retirement Offerings in the Fortune 500. USA: Towers Watson.

[26] Matthew Vickery, "This Italian Island Is Home to the Oldest People in the World. Here's Their Secret," *USA Today*, updated November 15, 2017, usatoday.com/story/news/world/2017/11/14/sardinia-oldest-people-world-italy/811783001.

[27] William A. Sadler, *The Third Age: Six Principles for Personal Growth and Rejuvenation After Forty* (Cambridge, MA: Da Capo Press, 2000).

[28] Clare Ansberry, "Bonne Bell Retires Stereotypes with Seniors-Only Department," *Wall Street Journal*, updated February 5, 2001, https://www.wsj.com/articles/SB981326619304234105.

29 Alice G. Walton, "What Are Your Regrets? Most People Regret Not Becoming 'Ideal Self,' Study Finds," *Forbes*, May 30, 2018, https://www.forbes.com/sites/alicegwalton/2018/05/30/what-are-your-regrets-most-people-regret-not-becoming-ideal-self-study-finds/#f8b06a24925e.

30 Timothy A. Pychyl, "What's Your 'Ought Self' Like?" *Psychology Today*, May 22, 2008, https://www.psychologytoday.com/us/blog/dont-delay/200805/whats-your-ought-self.

31 Irem Gunay, "Actual Self Versus Best Self," *Positive Psychology News*, April 27, 2013, https://positivepsychologynews.com/news/irem-gunay/2013042725817#; Zawn Villines, "Study: Regret About One's Ideal Self Often Hurts the Most," *Good Therapy*, June 15, 2018, https://www.goodtherapy.org/blog/study-regret-about-ones-ideal-self-often-hurts-most-0615181.

32 Amy Norton, "1 in 3 Young Adults Suffers from Loneliness in U.S.," *US News and World Report*, March 11, 2019, https://www.usnews.com/news/health-news/articles/2019-03-11/1-in-3-young-adults-suffers-from-loneliness-in-us.

33 Vern L. Bengtson, "Beyond the Nuclear Family: The Increasing Importance of Multigenerational Bonds," *Journal of Marriage and Family* 63 (February 2001): 1–16, https://doi.org/10.1111/j.1741-3737.2001.00001.x.

34 Brad Klontz, "Do You Have a Money Disorder?" *Psychology Today*, January 30, 2010, https://www.psychologytoday.com/us/blog/mind-over-money/201001/do-you-have-money-disorder.

35 Madeline Farber, "Nearly Two-Thirds of American Can't Pass a Basic Test of Financial Literacy," *Fortune*, July

12, 2016, https://fortune.com/2016/07/12/financial-literacy; Stephen J. Dubner, "Everything You Always Wanted to Know about Money (but Were Afraid to Ask)," *Freakonomics,* August 2, 2017, http://freakonomics.com/podcast/everything-always-wanted-know-money-afraid-ask.

[36] Dayana Yochim, "Study: Money Secrets and Sluggish Savings Put Couples' Retirement Dreams at Risk," *Nerd Wallet,* accessed November 20, 2019, https://www.nerdwallet.com/blog/investing/study-couples-keep-retirement-savings-secrets.

[37] Paul J. Yakoboski, "Worries and Plans as Individuals Approach Retirement," *Benefits Quarterly* 27 (2): 34–37, https://www.researchgate.net/publication/51070314_Worries_and_plans_as_individuals_approach_retirement .

[38] Chris Farrell, "The Truth about Health Care Costs in Retirement," *Forbes,* June 28, 2018, https://www.forbes.com/sites/nextavenue/2018/06/28/the-truth-about-health-care-costs-in-retirement/#5da9781b4401.

[39] Jean M. Lown, "Development and Validation of a Financial Self-Efficacy Scale," *Journal of Financial Counseling and Planning* 22 (January 2011), https://papers.ssrn.com/sol3/papers.cfm?abstract_id=2006665; Albert Bandura, *Self-Efficacy: The Exercise of Control* (New York: Worth Publishers, 1997).

[40] Lown, 2011.

[41] Miriam Akhtar, "What Is Self-Efficacy? Bandura's 4 Sources of Efficacy Beliefs," *Positive Psychology,* November 8, 2018, http://positivepsychology.org.uk/self-efficacy-definition-bandura-meaning.

[42] Gregg Lunceford, "Should Your Retirement Include Work?" *Forbes,* January 12, 2018, https://www.forbes.com/sites/forbesfinancecouncil/2018/01/12/should-your-retirement-include-work/#128ae83365ee.

[43] Sarah Stevenson, "University Based Retirement Communities," *Senior Living,* September 3, 2014, https://www.aplaceformom.com/blog/9-3-14-seniors-head-back-to-school.

[44] Retirement Living, "College-Linked Retirement Communities," accessed November 20, 2019, https://www.retirementliving.com/college-linked-retirement-communities.

[45] Carol Fishman Cohen, "Applying the Internship Model to Retirees," *Next Avenue,* January 27, 2017, https://www.nextavenue.org/internship-model-retirees.

[46] Randy Lilleston, "It's Never Too Late for an Internship," *AARP,* February 28, 2018, https://www.aarp.org/work/job-search/info-2018/internship-employment-gap-fd.html.

[47] Retire by Forty, "Why Join Peace Corps After Retirement," accessed November 20, 2019, https://retireby40.org/join-peace-corps-retirement.

[48] Kimberly Lankford, "Volunteer Abroad in the Peace Corps in Retirement," *Kiplinger,* August 6, 2018, https://www.kiplinger.com/article/retirement/T012-C000-S004-volunteer-abroad-in-the-peace-corps-in-retirement.html.

[49] Whitney Johnson, "Entrepreneurs Get Better with Age," *Harvard Business Review,* June 27, 2013, https://hbr.org/2013/06/entrepreneurs-get-better-with.

[50] Gregg Lunceford, "Entrepreneurship: The Retirement Solution," *Forbes,* April 9, 2018, https://www.forbes.com/sites/forbesfinancecouncil/2018/04/09/entrepreneurship-the-retirement-solution/#78b119920c66.

[51] Rachel Nauen, "Half of Mature U.S. Workers Will Wait Until At Least Age 70 to Retire or Won't Retire at All", Career Builder, March, 2017, http://press.careerbuilder.com/2017-03-31-Half-of-Mature-U-S-Workers-Will-Wait-Until-At-Least-Age-70-to-Retire-or-Wont-Retire-at-All

Made in the USA
Monee, IL
28 April 2023

32586657R00105